# Teach Smarter

"This is 'a book for teachers by a teacher', offering specific, practical advice on a range of subjects related to professional practice. It should be particularly useful for early career teachers who have completed their NQT year and who are beginning to find their way in the classroom. Adam Riches advises us to focus on 'doing simple things well', tweaking our practice in the light of your own context, and finding a sustainable balance so that we teach well without exhausting ourselves. He stresses the importance of continuing to ask 'how does that help learning?' and to strip back extraneous activity which takes time and energy without enhancing the pupils' experience.

"Throughout the book, Adam poses questions which encourage reflection and help the reader to engage with the ideas he is exploring. He structures his advice around Sweller's Cognitive Load Theory, Rosenshine's Principles of Instruction and Bjork's Desirable Difficulty. The elements of teaching he covers include: the importance of cultural literacy; the use of space in the classroom and ensuring you have a presence; the power of display to support learning; successful modelling; effective planning; clarity of expectations; judicious use of praise; engaging and working with parents; productive use of feedback; and skilful questioning. At all stages Adam is mindful of how we can ensure our efforts are reasonable and sustainable.

"His underpinning message? 'Knowing when enough is enough is the key to ensuring that you stay in the profession.'

"Reading this book should help teachers to become more efficient and effective. He encourages us to plan a change in practice which will help us to be better at our jobs and less likely to feel overwhelmed. He stresses the importance of being thoughtful and discriminating. 'You don't need to be critical, but you must critique your practice.' Reflective = effective, Adam suggests. This book should help teachers to teach well, to keep things in perspective and strive to find a balance in their lives so that they can thrive. It may stop some of them walking away from the classroom."

**Jill Berry**,
Leadership Consultant and former Headteacher, UK

"Teach smarter: what an alluring and powerful concept. When we enter a career as demanding and complex as teaching, it is this that we are desperately striving for. Those first few years often pass in a haze of confusion, late-night planning and sneering at any suggestion that we should have a 'work–life balance'. Luckily, for these overstretched and exhausted teachers, Adam Riches' book has arrived at exactly the right time. He provides us with utter clarity about how we can become more efficient in the classroom, using a wide range of educational research to support his excellent advice.

"I remember being desperate for clear, instantly transferable advice in my first few years of teaching. I would have devoured this book and I know it would have saved me a significant amount of time (and from making even more mistakes!). Now, over a decade into this wonderful profession, I left reading it feeling invigorated and with a range of new ideas to experiment with. The chapter on feedback has been a revolution for me – saving me time and helping my students understand how to improve. We are desperate to keep energised and motivated new teachers in the profession, and the advice nestled in this book will undoubtedly help to achieve this. It is time to reject the notion we should work harder and burn out, and instead embrace Adam's philosophy that we teach smarter and have more impact."

**Jamie Thom**,
English teacher and author of *Slow Teaching*

"This book from Adam Riches is incredibly timely. We have a retention crisis that drives far too many teachers out of the classroom early in their careers. I have no doubt that the sage advice in this book will do much to return some sanity to the profession and help keep teachers teaching."

**Mark Enser**,
teacher and author of *Teach Like Nobody's Watching*

"Retention of early career teachers is a current problem in education and in this book, Adam makes a number of practical and useful suggestions aimed at early career teachers about how they can take ownership of their professional practice and not become overwhelmed by the requirements of teaching in their first crucial years of teaching. Full of lots of practical advice as Adam is writing from his current context as a practising classroom teacher."

**Kate Sida-Nicholls**,
(FCCT) Suffolk and Norfolk SCITT Secondary
PGCE Course Leader

# Teach Smarter

As a teacher, the more efficient you are, the less stressful work becomes, and the more effective you are, the more you can focus on teaching those in front of you. *Teach Smarter* is an essential guide that helps early career teachers reduce their unnecessary workload by offering practical classroom strategies that can save you, and those you work with, time.

With a focus on keeping teaching simple and ensuring everything has a meaningful purpose, this book offers guidance on reducing workload through careful reflection and evaluation of your teaching practice. Offering ways to adjust your pedagogy and streamline your approaches in the classroom, *Teach Smarter* gives you more time to focus on what is important: helping your students progress. Questioning what it means to "teach smart", the chapters explore topics including:

- Planning
- Feedback
- Classroom space
- Expectations
- Reflecting on your teaching and managing stress

Written by an experienced classroom teacher, coach and mentor, this book is essential reading for trainee teachers, NQTs and RQTs.

**Adam Riches** is a full-time English teacher in the UK. He is a senior leader for teaching and learning and a specialist leader in education.

# Teach Smarter

## Efficient and Effective Strategies for Early Career Teachers

Adam Riches

LONDON AND NEW YORK

First published 2020
by Routledge
2 Park Square, Milton Park, Abingdon, Oxon OX14 4RN

and by Routledge
52 Vanderbilt Avenue, New York, NY 10017

*Routledge is an imprint of the Taylor & Francis Group, an informa business*

© 2020 Adam Riches

The right of Adam Riches to be identified as author of this work has been asserted by him in accordance with sections 77 and 78 of the Copyright, Designs and Patents Act 1988.

All rights reserved. No part of this book may be reprinted or reproduced or utilised in any form or by any electronic, mechanical, or other means, now known or hereafter invented, including photocopying and recording, or in any information storage or retrieval system, without permission in writing from the publishers.

*Trademark notice*: Product or corporate names may be trademarks or registered trademarks, and are used only for identification and explanation without intent to infringe.

*British Library Cataloguing-in-Publication Data*
A catalogue record for this book is available from the British Library

*Library of Congress Cataloging-in-Publication Data*
Names: Riches, Adam (Educator), author.
Title: Teach smarter: efficient and effective strategies for
early career teachers / Adam Riches.
Description: Abingdon, Oxon; New York, NY: Routledge, 2020. |
Includes bibliographical references and index.
Identifiers: LCCN 2019056995 (print) | LCCN 2019056996 (ebook) |
ISBN 9780367859855 (hardback) | ISBN 9780367859862 (paperback) |
ISBN 9781003016236 (ebook)
Subjects: LCSH: First year teachers. | Teachers–Workload.
Classification: LCC LB2844.1.N4 R55 2020 (print) |
LCC LB2844.1.N4 (ebook) | DDC 371.102–dc23
LC record available at https://lccn.loc.gov/2019056995
LC ebook record available at https://lccn.loc.gov/2019056996

ISBN: 9780367859855 (hbk)
ISBN: 9780367859862 (pbk)
ISBN: 9781003016236 (ebk)

Typeset in Melior
by Newgen Publishing UK

*For both the E.R.R.s in my life who keep my head up and keep my heart strong.*

# Contents

| | | |
|---|---|---:|
| | Introduction | 1 |
| 1 | What does it mean to teach smart? | 5 |
| | *Can I teach smart?* | 6 |
| | *The answer to everything* | 9 |
| | *Where's the research?* | 11 |
| | *What does it mean to be reflective?* | 11 |
| 2 | Smart theory (and wider ideas) | 13 |
| | *John Sweller – Cognitive Load Theory* | 14 |
| | *Barak Rosenshine – ten principles of instruction* | 17 |
| | *Robert Bjork – desirable difficulty* | 20 |
| | *Applying theory in a smart way* | 22 |
| | *Wider ideas* | 24 |
| 3 | Classroom space | 29 |
| | *Classroom layout* | 30 |
| | *The desks* | 31 |
| | *The pupils* | 33 |
| | *The displays* | 35 |
| | *Desk or no desk?* | 37 |
| | *Why is it so important to consider your space?* | 39 |
| 4 | Planning | 45 |
| | *What to plan* | 46 |
| | *Talking* | 48 |

|   |   |   |
|---|---|---|
|   | *Modelling* | 52 |
|   | *Being responsive – the art of winging it* | 55 |
|   | *Sharing the load* | 56 |
| 5 | Expectations | 59 |
|   | *Just behaviour?* | 60 |
|   | *Less can be more* | 61 |
|   | *Clarity is key* | 62 |
|   | *Engagement* | 63 |
|   | *Consistency* | 65 |
|   | *Praise* | 67 |
|   | *Parents* | 70 |
|   | *Expectations of teachers* | 72 |
| 6 | Feedback | 75 |
|   | *Making the distinction between marking and feedback* | 77 |
|   | *Monitoring tasks* | 79 |
|   | *Live feedback* | 81 |
|   | *Whole-class feedback* | 84 |
|   | *Peer feedback* | 87 |
| 7 | Questioning | 91 |
|   | *Subject knowledge* | 93 |
|   | *Distribution* | 94 |
|   | *Commonality of language* | 96 |
|   | *Using the right type of question* | 97 |
| 8 | Reflecting | 109 |
|   | *Plan/prepare/implement/reflect/repeat* | 109 |
|   | *Keep on keeping on* | 110 |
|   | *Read up* | 112 |
|   | *Manage stress* | 113 |
|   | *Final words* | 114 |
|   | References | 115 |
|   | Index | 119 |

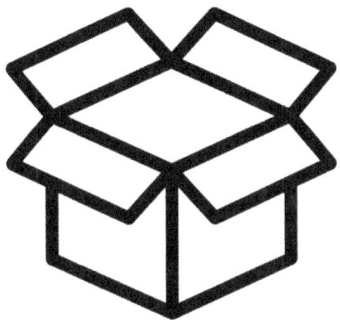

# Introduction

Teaching is a complex craft. It can be time-consuming, stressful and at times unbearable, but the pressure of the job, for most, is offset by the reward of helping learners overcome difficulties and succeed in their own individual ways.

Whatever your motivations for teaching, I think everyone can agree that the more efficient you are, the less stressful work becomes, and the more effective you are, the more you are able to teach those in front of you what you need to (in the somewhat limited time given).

## Nobody said it was easy...

As an early career teacher in this day and age, the pressure is incredible. Leaving aside external factors, balancing the day-to-day duties of being a classroom practitioner is a tough gig. Planning, marking, giving feedback, assessing and engaging learners isn't easy at the best of times and that's without eating, sleeping and maybe talking to people who aren't teachers about something that isn't to do with education (turns out non-teachers don't like talking about effective feedback – who knew?). The first years of your career are when you do your real training and teachers are increasingly, and understandably, buckling under the pressure. ITT providers have a year to prepare teachers for battle in the classroom and it isn't until those first lessons where you're off the proverbial leash that you realise the true pressures of being a teacher.

## Not all habits are bad habits

Getting yourself established in habits that are effective isn't easy, or we'd all be stress-free. There are a number of factors that inhibit effective and efficient practice. First and foremost, schools are historically traditional establishments. This means that it can be difficult for new teachers to not be imprinted on by the old guard or the establishment in which they teach. It's totally natural, and it's also equally as hard for new teachers to have their voices heard. The traditional nature of most schools means that to have your voice heard, you often have to have to have put in some time before others hear you. It can be frustrating. Second, in an age in which it is easy to access information, there is almost too much literature on how to be an effective teacher. Some of the fads pass, some stay and some go unnoticed – regardless, it can be hard to know which pieces of information to take on-board and what is white noise. Finally, and I'd say most importantly, as an early career teacher, you don't get enough guidance or time to reflect on what you do and sometimes more importantly what your school does. This can be an issue for two reasons: number one, you plateau in your teaching and become demotivated because instead of becoming more effective, you keep doing what you've always done and end up doing more of it; and two you don't prepare yourself for the next step of your career where you need to have a bigger picture and a better idea of how things work and why they do (or don't) lead to success. I'm hoping this book will help out.

## Honest advice

I'm no expert when it comes to researching and I'm certainly no super academic – I'm just a normal guy who teaches kids stuff... and teaches teachers a few things too. I've been an English teacher for nine years and I've had the privilege of working alongside hundreds of trainees in various ITT capacities. I'm a Senior Leader for teaching learning in my current role and I'm Head of English. I have a 60% timetable and I work four days a week. On average, I have minus time each week – we all know how time-intensive schools can be and the context in which I teach is a challenge. That's why it's so important for me to work effectively – I'm not in a school that is easy and I'm not in the business of coasting. I enjoy working, but I don't enjoy stress and my one aim across all of my various roles is to keep the workload for me, and the teachers around me, at a level that allows them to fulfil their job in a way that also allows them to function outside of school.

## Workload… and books?

Workload is a funny thing. Individuals have their own self-imposed and organisationally imposed pressures. I've written this book in a way that I hope teachers can use it to reflect on how they can reduce their workload in their own contexts through self- and shared efficacy. Taking into account the stark differences between schools, I realise that reducing workload isn't a one-size-fits-all formula. My concept is that this book will allow you to look at what you do, look at what your school does and in light of these two factors, consider what you can do inside the parameters you work within and make changes that allow you to reduce your workload and help you become more efficient. I also hope that this reflection will allow you, as early career teachers, to more effectively put forth strategies to help others in reducing their workload.

So many education books for teachers are written by extremely experienced retired teachers, teachers who have moved on to training at HE establishments or those who have ventured into (the somewhat foggy) world of consultation. The ideas are theoretically sound but quite often by default are de-contextualised and although amazing in theory, are difficult to apply in their full form in reality. This book is different. I'm in the trenches, I'm teaching four lessons each day and I'm practising what I preach. I don't want to take anything away from anyone else, but this quite categorically is a book *for* teachers *by* a teacher. It has been designed in a way that allows you to engage with the content, reflect on what you do now, have a think, reflect on what your school does, have another think, and then take the pieces you can and implement them in your context in a way that allows you to become more effective.

To maintain the focus on low workload, I've only included content that I believe will help reduce the time you spend working, giving you the tools to keep your head clear to focus on good quality teaching. The topics start off broadly and then filter into much more specific areas of teaching and pedagogy. At first, the book will help you begin to be reflective on how you can strip back your teaching to focus on what is most important in the classroom. This is followed by the underpinning theories which I think are absolutely paramount to successfully reducing your workload, with again the opportunity to reflect on how you can embed these approaches into your teaching. Then we get onto the proper stuff – adapting your practice to become more effective and efficient, regardless of your constraints and parameters. The focus begins on ensuring your space is set up to allow you to succeed, before moving to planning, the importance of expectations and how you can effectively feed-back to students without spending hours marking books. Questioning is explored and different approaches evaluated before the final chapter encourages you to look at your practice holistically and consider what you can take away.

I wholeheartedly hope that this book helps you reduce stress, enjoy your teaching more and I also hope it gives you more free time to do what you want to do in your life, because teaching is the best job in the world... if we can do away with some of the weight!

# 1 What does it mean to teach smart?

Do the simple things right.

Teaching smart isn't something that fits into a neat box. For any teacher to truly master their craft, they need to be self-reflective – the more reflective you become, the more effective you are as a teacher. In short, reflective = effective. Teaching smart is about stripping back the white noise, doing away with the unnecessary frills and frolics and focusing in on doing the simple things right. Doing the simple things well is of paramount importance, as these cornerstones will provide the pillars for you to build your teaching upon.

If you look at classroom craft, we can do some rudimentary division so we have some subsections – it's difficult because a lot of the areas overlap (quite significantly in some cases), but if we take the elements of an exceptional lesson, we'll need to think about the following:

- Understanding

- Classroom

- Planning
- Expectations
- Feedback
- Questioning

This book will look at each of these areas in detail and help you reflect on how you can adapt your practice to include them, without adding additional burden to you already busy job. Hopefully, you'll find sharpening and mastering these elements will hugely reduce your workload.

Spinning these plates is tricky, especially when there are so many other factors in the classroom (not to mention the 30 students sat in front of you) which can have a huge impact on your lessons. Teaching smart is all about harnessing your skills and working on areas of your teaching that you identify as less effective than others. There is no book or paper that has all of the answers to reducing workload, but by building teachers' confidence in their ability to self-regulate we are able to reduce the impact that ineffectual practice has.

We could of course break teaching down into hundreds of separate elements... but that wouldn't encourage truly smart teaching. There are reams and reams of pages that focus on different teaching approaches that improve outcomes, but none of these approaches focus on the importance of tweaking your own practice in light of your own context. Often, reading about how to overcome a problem you have faced (especially early in your career) can be more demotivating than supportive, especially if the research was conducted or the idea born in a context very different from your own.

Reflecting on what you do and how you do it is a much more effective way of working. It's simple really.

## Can I teach smart?

Anyone can teach smart. The whole point is that it doesn't have to be rocket science.

For some, in an ideal world, there would be no constraints in the classroom. For others, constraints allow a level of consistency and confidence. Modifying our own practice can often be shaped by the context in which we teach. Wherever you are, let me assure you that you do have a say in how you teach. Policy, approach and ethos all contribute to constraints on how teachers can go about their jobs.

These institutional constraints often limit how much individualism a teacher can exhibit. By this I mean depending on your context, your leadership may be more instructionalist, constraining approaches centrally, or if your school is more established (and often has a longer track record of success), leadership may be more transactional. Regardless of the levels of freedom, each with their own merits, classroom teachers can modify their practice and delivery to be smarter.

Teaching smarter doesn't just mean doing less. It means working more efficiently. Sometimes, that can mean working less (obviously) but more often it means thinking about why something is being done and considering if it is necessary. The process can be really empowering and once you've had a chance to look at individual elements of your practice, simplify them and streamline them, you'll find that you can apply the same approaches to more complex areas of teaching… it doesn't take long for this to spread. Whichever point you're at on the ladder in school, we all intrinsically want to make things as effective as possible, for ourselves, for the kids and for others we work with.

Some of the ideas that you will come across (in this book or generally throughout your career) will meet stiff opposition. That's life. Something I learnt early on in my teaching career was that if you truly believe in something then you need to pursue it in the right way. In schools especially, change can be slow and opposed with fury. It's not something you seem to see in other industries, but coming back to the ideas of "traditionally" run schools, you often run into the, "Well I've never done it like that and I'm alright" attitude, or my other personal favourite, "That's not what I was taught when I was training [ten years ago]…". In short, some teachers think it'll be more work changing their ways than ploughing on with what they know. Maybe that's why things take so long to change in some schools. My advice is don't be disheartened. If they don't want to change, that's great, but that doesn't stop you looking at your own practice. It's only a matter of time… trust me.

Although it is important to be clear about what makes good pedagogy (James & Pollard, 2011), we must also relate this to something that is tangible and at every point possible to ensure that we aren't just highlighting what needs changing and adding to the problem. With this in mind, I have tried to couple a way to reduce workload through effective pedagogy or organisation to every workload issue highlighted – just like in our lessons, we need to provide the *how*, not just the *why*.

## How are we at this point?

Education is a field that is in a constant state of flux. Often, schools and education are the showpiece of political rhetoric – the outcome, of course, is an ever-changing landscape of pressures and targets that need to be achieved on an ever-more restricted budget and timescale. At the bottom of this is us: the teachers who actually do the teaching.

In a lot of ways (weirdly) schooling hasn't changed much in Britain from its original conception. In fact there are practices that we saw 150 years ago that are still present in the classroom today (we'll talk about some of these later) and most notably, there is still a teacher who teaches.

Many things have changed since the Victorian times – thankfully for most – but the concept of schooling remains the same: teach kids some stuff. The transference of knowledge from an expert to a nonexpert with some element of formalised teaching and a test at the end to ascertain how much knowledge has been learned. The issue is that society's expectation of teachers has not remained constant. In turn, the pressure on those who are in the classroom has been cranked up and as we as a society become progressively more results-driven, the responsibility of those doing the teaching increases.

I've been in education for a decade or so and even in that short space of time the temperature of teaching has changed. The debate that has raged on (for longer than my career) has been the workload of teachers – the expectations of the government, of parents and, of course, of leaders in school seem to have a direct impact on everyone in the classroom. Some absolutely phenomenal teachers have left the profession in this time, and even more worryingly, they've not been replaced because in short, people see what teaching entails and don't want to train. The knock-on impact of this is that the supply of new teachers has started to dry up and even with new teachers entering the profession, some are opting out of teaching after a few years. This is triggering a retention crisis and if we are worried about workload now, it's going to be a whole lot worse when there aren't enough staff to go around.

Over-complication of policy and a lack of will to move away from deep-rooted traditions are often to blame for the direct workload impact on teachers, especially those entering the profession. Teaching on the face of it isn't an easy job and just because you get the holidays doesn't mean you actually get holidays. For most, the time away from school is needed for their own mental stability and for some, the holiday just means more work.

As the government works on making some nice new posters about how teachers can reduce their workload, it falls to us in the classroom to both get the results and to find a balance that is sustainable. In recent years, there has been a boom in pedagogy and sharing of good practice and as history has repeatedly proved, in times of great need there is great innovation (or in some cases great finding of old stuff that was amazing but not noticed – Rosenshine is a great example) and although things can seem bleak at times, there are great beams of light piercing through the clouds.

The proverbial light is shining brighter in some places than others and in those places there are some clear elements of practice that are allowing teachers to reduce their workload. Heightened consistency, research-informed approaches and shared efficacy are all elements that we often see, but when you drill down in any school with content staff, at the core is the fact that they do their job well. They are effective at teaching and they are allowed to be.

## The answer to everything

When anyone asks what the solution is for pretty much any classroom situation, the answer quite often is quality-first teaching; the concept of stripping back everything and focusing on how the students learn. Get rid of the gimmicks, simplify everything and get the basics right. SEN, pupil premium, EAL, it doesn't matter – putting quality teaching first will trump almost any incentive, training or investment.

Putting the quality of your teaching first is how you teach smart. Stripping everything away and going simple may seem counter-intuitive, especially early in your career as a teacher, but start how you mean to go on. Any time you are going to do something – be it extra work, an assessment, a course – ask yourself these questions:

- What impact will this have on my students' learning?
- Could I be doing something else?
- Will doing this save me time in the long run?
- Can I do this in another way?

If you're struggling to answer any of the above, then you might want to rethink why you are doing what you are.

By being reflective and thinking smart, you can quickly filter out any work that is futile and in turn reduce your workload significantly... but it doesn't stop there. A lot of teachers are teaching in contexts where they follow the traditions of those before them, as we've ascertained. Specifications change, schools become academies and Education Secretaries come and go, but teachers are still often entrapped by traditions and expectations that quite simply are ineffective. By being more reflective and becoming more effective in your own practice, you are able to coach and guide others to do the same for themselves. Without exaggerating too much, the more you are able to reduce your own workload, the more equipped you are to do so for those around you.

The tide needs to turn in education for us to retain teachers entering the profession, and ensuring that you get your own practice secured early in your career means that you last for longer. Removing the opposition from their well-fortified trenches isn't achieved by force, instead it's achieved by the realisation that they don't have to work every weekend and holiday and that to get good results they don't have to put on morning, lunch and twilight sessions.

## Where's the research?

Interestingly, the educational world is now relatively inundated with research around effective teaching and learning. The problem is that this spike in "research" has led to a muddying of the waters around practice in the classroom. There is no doubt that there is a wealth of amazing classroom-based research out there, alongside a load of exceptional educational psychology and work on cognition, but it's not always easy to pick out the fool's gold, especially early in your career.

One of the issues faced by teachers is that research (like so much advice on teaching) is de-contextualised and therefore only gives a snapshot of a very particular setting. Often in education, studies will be conducted with small groups and suddenly a new theory will be announced. The issue is that research can be as dangerous as it is useful.

There are a few questions you may want to ask of any research that you come across:

- What is the bias of the researcher?
- How big is the study?
- Who funded the research
- What does it actually show?

If you're satisfied after the above, you may want to proceed.

Something else to consider when it comes to research is how you use it.

Interestingly, as long as you're informed, educational research can be a real tool – but don't always take it at face value. Workload can be hugely increased if we as teachers, or those above us, misinterpret the message that the study is sending. Unless you conduct your own research in your school or trust, you need to be aware of the dangers of relying on individual studies.

## What does it mean to be reflective?

The ability to look at your own practice and think about what you could do to improve it is a real skill. If you also factor in how busy teachers are generally, sometimes self-reflection isn't high on the priority list, especially if you are treading water on a number of fronts.

Teacher training providers are excellent at getting trainees to reflect on the teaching, their observations and their general time at school by embedding it into courses. Once you've qualified, however, reflection awkwardly crops up at CPD sessions a few times a year for most. To reduce your workload, you need to be able to identify what is effective and what isn't in your teaching. If you don't do this, you might be making ineffective changes to your practice and this is exactly what we are trying to avoid.

There are four dimensions of teaching that we can reflect on as suggested by Danielson (2007): planning and preparation, classroom environment, instruction and professional responsibilities – the content of this book is mostly based around these four areas (in one guise or another). If we take the time to look at these areas individually, as teachers, we are able to hone our practice in a way that allows sustainable growth. Simply "reflecting on your teaching" is a job that is too broad and too vague to have any real impact.

Reflecting can take many forms and, in reality, just the thought process can be enough for the basis for self-improvement. Taking the time to look at students' work in lessons, think about what the learners responded to and what they didn't is all part of ensuring your teaching stays as effective as possible. Making the changes you need to is what makes you efficient. It isn't always a comfortable process looking at how you teach, but by critiquing (not criticising) you are quickly able to ascertain areas of strength and areas that need some attention.

Throughout this book, I've placed (very strategically) some reflective questions to help you engage with the ideas in a way that makes them relevant to you. Some of the concepts I talk about may already align with what you do, some may differ vastly, but taking the time to think about why things work or don't work in your context will allow you to make some executive decisions about what you do in the classroom.

Self-efficacy is a skill that means you are able to develop yourself. If you can develop yourself, you are able to move your teaching forward at a much higher rate than someone who is less aware of themselves.

# 2 Smart theory (and wider ideas)

Educational research and educational theories can be overwhelmingly complicated and yield underwhelming results in the classroom. For early career teachers, it can be difficult filtering through the literature and picking out what really works. With your workload in the classroom, you also may lack the inclination to pour over academic papers, articles and other such word-dense materials when you could be… well, doing literally anything else.

With that said, having a sound pedagogical knowledge base is paramount for reducing your workload. If you can master the basics of learning, your teaching becomes more efficient; in turn, your workload is reduced. But what are the basics of learning? For me, there are three main ideas and theories that make up the basics of learning and these three things combined are responsible for the vast majority of successful teaching and learning policies. It's a huge statement, but I truly believe that by mastering the concepts in these three theories, you can successfully underpin your teaching with efficient and effective pedagogy.

There are, of course, an exhaustive list of people who could make the cut here, but the three theorists that I have chosen work together in unison to reduce the complexity of teaching and learning in order to get the most out of children – for me, they ring perfectly true for the theme and aim of this book.

So, if I was to have my hypothetical learning tea party (and what a party it would be), I'd invite the late Barak Rosenshine, John Sweller and Robert Bjork. Between the three of them, they are able to effectively encapsulate anything you need to know with regard to effective and efficient practice. The whole of this book in fact can be related in some way to the thoughts and findings of these three people.

## John Sweller – Cognitive Load Theory

Cognitive Load Theory (CLT) for me has been huge. John Sweller's original 1988 and his subsequent 1998 paper on the concept, in a nutshell, were the biggest influencing factors on the way I teach today. It's a bold claim, but I'd say they're the most important papers I have read with regard to pedagogy and the understanding of teaching and learning. And it's not just me – a few years ago, Dylan Wiliam tweeted that he had "come to the conclusion Sweller's Cognitive Load Theory is the single most important thing for teachers to know". Without exaggeration, Sweller's original findings now form the backbone to the theory behind a lot of my teaching.

The concept behind the theory is incredibly simple (and hugely complex at the same time) and in some ways commonsensical, but Sweller's words have had a huge impact across the world.

CLT is based around the idea that our working memory can only deal with a limited amount of information at one time. The theory focuses on the significance of how our brains deal with stimulus or inputs, breaking down the concept that new information needs to be fed to learners in a way that allows them to process it without being overburdened.

Sweller's theory identifies three different types of cognitive load:

1. Intrinsic cognitive load: The inherent difficulty of the material itself (which can be influenced by prior knowledge of the topic)

2. Extraneous cognitive load: The load generated by the way the material is presented and which does not aid learning

3. Germane cognitive load: The elements that aid information processing and contribute to the development of "schemas".

In short, Sweller's papers highlight the flaws of overloading our working memory and the impact that has on the completion of tasks and, more importantly, the transferring of information from our short-term, finite working memory to our theoretically infinite long-term memory.

So theory aside, why will these papers have such an impact on your teaching? It's simple really, CLT gives you a firm understanding of how brains work in layman's terms. Sweller's papers explain learning from a psychological point of view in a way that you, as a totally normal classroom practitioner, can understand. The advantage of this is that you can make active decisions when planning to ensure that learners aren't overloaded with unnecessary inputs and stimulus that may overburden them and that may have inhibited learning and progress in the past.

The impact of Sweller's papers will be instantly notable in your lessons. I can almost guarantee every task you do, everything you say, every question you ask will in some way be linked to the concepts put forth by Sweller. Most of the approaches which I now adopt are directly derived from these findings, if not they are influenced or inspired by elements of Cognitive Load Theory. Think of a few of the big names at the moment… any of this theory ring any bells? It's present in so much of the literature that's available on pedagogy. My advice, however, is to go to the source.

### How will this help?

By understanding cognitive load, I've been able to adopt a number of tricks in my teaching to ensure that learners are able to access the information I'm trying to get across to them. I know that intrinsic cognitive load can be reduced by breaking down the subject content, sequencing the delivery into small chunks so that pieces are taught individually before being explained together as a whole – it makes absolute sense to teach in this way, but CLT makes this kind of an approach make sense; for me, it answers the question I'm always asking – "why does that help learning?" In your classroom, CLT helps you think through your tasks and make the planning you do significantly more effective and, in turn, the learning in your classes becomes more efficient.

I think something that I was a bit ignorant of before reading the paper is the impact of extraneous cognitive load – obviously because I didn't know it existed. Excessive extraneous load can be attributed to at least 90% of the issues I faced when I first started teaching... but I didn't know that. I made cards, I did whizzy things with PPT and I read books on behaviour. The irony is that by adopting these approaches I was exacerbating the issue! Throwing in more variables to an already overloaded learner's brain isn't a good approach – but I didn't know any better. Don't make the same mistakes that I made.

My understanding of how learners process new material by referencing schema or mental models of pre-existing knowledge means that I know that clearer is better. Where I'd previously tried to find a solution, Sweller made me realise that one of the highest impact factors on new learning is actually lack of clarity in instruction due to the increased load on the working memory. A good example might be a lesson that uses a PPT with a lot of text on it and the teacher talking at the same time, this can inadvertently generate excessive cognitive load and lead to working memory overload. Again, it seems obvious now, but I look back at when I started teaching and my initial reaction to blank looks was to explain a concept again, but with different words, which is counterproductive.

### Apply the concepts right

There are, of course, potential issues with CLT and there are doubters, and that's to be expected. Reif (2010) writes that if cognitive load is reduced too much then learning essentially becomes too fragmented. Holton (2009) points out that it is difficult to measure cognitive load, and therefore difficult to generate evidence to prove the theory. In short there are cynics, but I'm not a cognitive scientist, I'm a teacher and I really like that there is a theory that has allowed me some insight into how minds may work.

The key things to consider and apply in lessons are as follows:

1. Break down subject content when introducing new topics and make time to recap and recall information.

2. Present instructions clearly without introducing too much information at the same time.

3. Be wary of reducing cognitive load too much – you don't want the desirable difficulty to be too low.

If you consider the factors above, you'll heighten engagement and you'll instantly see an increase in the opt-in during tasks. Something that amazes me about CLT is that it makes total sense and having an awareness of its power is something that can be a real tool in your classroom

Consideration of CLT can be as complex or as simple as you want it to be. On a lesson or even a task level, you may ask yourself:

- Am I getting a student to do two things with their brain at once?
- Are my resources cluttered or simple?
- Is what I have put on my PPT necessary?
- What can I do to keep my students' attention on the key idea?
- Have I given sufficient time for recalling and recapping of knowledge?
- Am I challenging my students?

## Barak Rosenshine – ten principles of instruction

Barak Rosenshine wrote his original paper on the six principles of instruction in the 1980s. The original can be traced back as far as a typed paper submitted to a US conference in 1982 – there's something quite amazing about seeing it in its typewritten glory. The then six "Instructional Functions" are extremely similar to the ten principles of instruction we know (and love) today.

Rosenshine's principles (2010, 2012) are nothing more than exceptionally good teaching techniques that teachers can adopt to ensure that their instructional practice is varied, targeted and effective. In short, the principles don't tell us anything new, but what they do is consolidate what good teaching looks like into digestible chunks. No faff, no gimmicks, just good instruction... and that's why understanding them is so important for all early career teachers.

The magic of Rosenshine's principles are that they are applicable to all teachers of all subjects and contexts – they focus on skills that teachers need to be successful in the classroom. From a pedagogical point of view, all of the aspects of the teacher standards are addressed or at least can be related to the individual principles – in short, Rosenshine encapsulates how to effectively teach in a very clever nutshell. All of this means that the approaches put forth are not subject-specific, the theory and thinking behind each principle can be applied no matter what you teach. What's more, the paper exemplifies how each approach can be utilised and applied in a classroom context.

Like all good pedagogical theory, Rosenshine's principles are underpinned by classroom practice. Rosenshine makes direct links between research, theory and classroom practice – each of the ten principles are presented in two parts: first, the research findings and then how these can be seen or done in the classroom. The success of the ten principles of instruction comes from their overwhelming simplicity and logic – straightforward, researched teaching that actually works in the classroom and, most importantly, doesn't add to teacher workload. Moreover, the way in which the paper is written (like Sweller's papers) is accessible to normal classroom teachers.

### Not *just* good teaching

Getting how learning actually works is something that any teacher needs to understand. What makes Rosenshine's principles so valuable to early career teachers is the way that it links real-life classroom practice to more complex ideas surrounding cognitive psychology. Understanding the process of learning is something that is pivotal to mastering effective teaching. Again, the simplicity of the practical strategies suggested exemplify that these approaches are applicable to all subjects.

Too often ideas are packaged in a way that makes them inaccessible, or by people who themselves are so far detached from the classroom, they have forgotten what it is like to teach real students. What resonates so much with Rosenshine's research is that it is often based on linking classroom observations to student outcomes, and the examples he gives show that he knows what children and teachers actually do. Not only that, Rosenshine writes in a way that encourages development. It isn't rigid advice, it makes you think and it makes you reflect – two things that are vital for newly qualified teachers who have recently flown the proverbial nest.

Regardless of how you were trained or the route you chose to get into teaching, to be a truly outstanding teacher, you need to be able to reflect and adapt your practice in order to make your teaching better. Rosenshine's principles give you the language to do that. The Teacher Standards are heavy and cumbersome for qualified teachers and they don't give that sharp focus for sharpening practice – they're too wordy and vague.

### Don't use them all at once

Rosenshine's principles of instruction are a guide to how to effectively include elements and phases in lessons that make your teaching more effective. Avoid thinking that a good lesson will contain every approach noted. I think one of the best ways to engage with Rosenshine is to not think of the principles as a recipe, think of them as more of a number of potential ingredients that can be combined depending on need. If you try to do too much, you'll negate the simplicity and create more extraneous load. From our understanding of CLT, the whole point is that our planning needs to keep this to a minimum.

Reflecting on your practice can focus around the principles. When planning, think about if you have exploited opportunities to include each of the principles of instruction, where relevant of course. Here are Rosenshine's ten principles of instruction:

1. Daily review
2. New material in small steps
3. Questioning

4. Provide models

5. Guide student practice

6. Check understanding

7. Obtain a high success rate

8. Scaffold difficult tasks

9. Independent practice

10. Weekly and monthly review

The likeness is that you will have included elements of some of the above naturally. By making a conscious effort to include the different approaches, you are able to improve your instructional practice in a sustainable and clear way. The simplicity of the principles allows you a common language to share too, with reduced space for ambiguity and confusion, and in addition you are able to look at individual elements of your planning and refine them if you want to.

Using Rosenshine's principles when planning allows you to ensure that your teaching is well supported and that students' learning is structured and sustainable. It's just smart.

## Robert Bjork – desirable difficulty

One of the theories that I think is most difficult to apply effectively is that of Robert Bjork. Bjork's concept of desirable difficulties suggests that introducing different levels of difficulty into learning significantly improves recall, retention and general memory performance. By ensuring that learning is pitched to a "desirable difficulty" teachers are able to stretch learners enough to be able to help them progress. If the difficulty isn't desirable, it is likely that the learners won't progress as well they potentially could (Bjork & Bjork, 2011).

Naturally, getting the pitch of a lesson right is a difficult task in itself. We as teachers often seek solace in student success and the idea of challenging students to the degree that they may not succeed straight away can be a daunting concept for an early career teacher. Learning isn't an easy thing to do, and at times getting students to engage may seem like a worry. You need to make the most of your lesson time without a minute wasted and in order to do this, you need to ensure that your planning doesn't include tasks that require minimal effort or brain power. Instead, tasks should be planned for the right degree of success. Patti Shank (2017) explains that "making learning too easy leads to thinking that learning has occurred when participants quickly forget and cannot actually apply". Moreover, Shank remind us that the more critical factor is in fact the application of the skill. Your planning shouldn't mean that all students succeed 100% of the time. On an individual level, the desirable difficulty for any individuals should be around 80% – mostly successful, but they get stuck and need to think on a deeper level before succeeding fully.

Jeffrey Bye (2011) draws on multiple research, suggesting the following methods for introducing desirable difficulties:

- Spacing learning sessions apart rather than massing them together (Baddeley & Longman, 1978; Dempster, 1990).

- Testing learners on material rather than having them simply restudy it (Roediger & Karpicke, 2006).

- Having learners generate target material through a puzzle or other kind of active process, rather than simply reading it passively (McDaniel et al., 1994).

- Varying the settings in which learning takes place (Smith et al., 1978).

- Making learning material less clearly organised (McNamara et al., 1996).

The whole point is that any of the above approaches add in extra proverbial hurdles for the learner in your class to jump over and, in turn, the difficulty of a task or series of tasks is increased.

If there is no difficulty, learners never adjust to having obstacles in their learning and do not build a resilience. Bye (2011) succinctly summarises: "Making learning too easy and straightforward can cause a misleading boost in the retrieval strength without causing the deeper processing that encourages the long-term retention afforded by higher storage strength." Simply, this exemplifies the importance of getting the pitch right. Success in the short term can build your confidence and make you think that your teaching is effective, but ensuring a good level of challenge means that you are more likely to help learners succeed in the long run. Don't be lulled into a false sense of security.

The aim is deeper processing of material through guided instruction. Avoiding making learning too easy seems counterintuitive to most early career teachers, especially as the whole concept of CLT seems to contradict this, but look at the theories closely. CLT doesn't make learning easier, it just highlights the pitfalls of working memory being overloaded. Desirable difficulty deals with the idea that a task needs to engage the learner's brain beyond the routine to build stronger schema. Again, the message is that easy learning means visible short-term gains but this does not translate to long-term memory retention.

- Do you know how hard your tasks really are?
- Have you been measuring success by how many students can "do it"?
- How can you increase the desirable difficulty in your lessons?
- Are there opportunities in your lessons where you can embed testing of knowledge explicitly?
- When can you get students to work through problems in your lessons?

Accessing the deeper thinking that is required for long-term learning to take place is a fine balancing act. Having an understanding and a handle of difficulty and how it can be manipulated to ensure that outcomes sustainably improve is key to making your teaching and the learning of your students more efficient,

## Applying theory in a smart way

Fads come and go. I've tried to focus the theory here on ideas that, if used effectively, will form the cornerstones of every element of your teaching. There is a tendency in education to jump onto the next big idea and forget those that came before it. For me, these ideas have withstood the test of time and will reduce your workload by changing the way you look at learning.

With any theory or idea that you come across in teaching, be it published or from a colleague, think objectively about it before trying to implement it in your practice. Consider if the approach will increase your workload and if so, is the increase representative of the gains that you are getting back with regard to the learners in your classes? Thinking smart about theory in itself reduces your workload.

There will inevitably be whole-school incentives that you will be expected to use or attempt to use in your teaching. My advice for these is similar. Consider how best to manipulate any idea to allow yourself to get the most from your classes. The likelihood is that the idea will stem from one of the three mentioned above.

When you come across research, articles or literature about improving or changing your teaching, put your thinking head on and reflect on more than just what is written. Some factors to consider might be the following:

- Who has written what you are reading? Are they a teacher?
- Does the research or theory have any bias?
- What else has the writer written about?
- Is the research or approach controversial? If so, why?
- Do you think what is being written about can be used in a real classroom?
- Are there any real-world examples of the approach or research findings in practice?

Depending on your answers to the above, you will be able to sift out some gems from the weighty stones. What's important is that you get something usable out of the reading you are doing. When it comes to workload, there are no silver bullets – mindlessly searching for them in reams of literature will just increase your workload.

## Wider ideas

In broader terms, we do need to consider some wider factors other than just the theoretical if we are to successfully embed exceptional practice into our classrooms.

If you aren't familiar with the concept of cultural capital, it's essentially to do with a person's knowledge about the world around them; in short, how much you know about stuff that's going on or has gone on in the world. As teachers, it isn't just our job to teach our subjects, we also play a huge part in making children into well-rounded human beings. No matter your context, the experiences you give your students will be adding to their cultural literacy... you may not being doing it consciously and that's why it's so important to be aware of how significant it is, because you're much more likely to include elements of it in your teaching if you do.

E.D. Hirsch in *Cultural Literacy* (Hirsch et al., 1988) succinctly summarises: "To be culturally literate is to possess the basic information needed to thrive in the modern world." It follows, therefore, that as teachers, we need to ensure that along with teaching the content of the curriculum, we are enabling students to function as well-informed individuals well after they leave school. It's a huge job, but without the guidance of their teachers, some young people have very little cultural input from elsewhere and therefore may miss opportunities others are able to access and make decisions that are less informed than they could be. Now more than ever, the job of the classroom teacher is of high importance.

I was privileged to have been able to hear a rather inspiring keynote speaker at an event recently who reminded me just how important it is for us, as educators, to keep in mind the importance of cultural capital in our teaching of young people. Jennifer Webb is a phenomenally inspiring teacher (and person) and her words really resonated with me and the context in which I teach. In areas of social deprivation, we see a significant dip in cultural capital and this can have a huge impact on students. To improve social mobility, we need to ensure that our teaching, across any demographic, takes into account the importance of the rich cultural tapestry that makes up life. But it isn't just students from deprived areas who need help understanding different experiences and understanding of contexts unfamiliar to their own, it's all children.

## What is cultural capital and where does it come from?

It is widely accepted that a person's level of cultural capital is a huge indicator of how well they are able to succeed academically and engage in wider society. This isn't a new concept and Ofsted certainly didn't coin it (although some people are only just starting to recognise it because it is mentioned in the Inspection Framework). French sociologist Pierre Bourdieu originally came up with the concept. Bourdieu (1973, 1986) explores the theory of cultural capital and highlights the link between an individual's background and their access to knowledge. Bourdieu (1986) breaks capital into three distinct types; embodied cultural capital, objectified capital and institutional cultural capital. Bourdieu emphasised that cultural capital is intrinsically linked to economic and social capital. Access to economic and social capital allows a higher access to cultural capital and Bourdieu (1973) observed that as a side-effect, cultural capital is often linked to social class and, as a result, re-enforced social divisions, hierarchies of power and inequality within society. Within education, we obviously aim to reduce and in time eradicate inequalities, but improving an individual student's cultural capital isn't a matter of giving somebody a book or sending them to see a play. And in turn, building on their social capital doesn't just mean giving them a talking frame so they know how to interact. There is much more to it. So how can we ensure that we build up the cultural and social capital of our students?

## Experiences

First, and most importantly, we can provide students with experiences. It doesn't have to be trips (of course, budgets are often tight) but ensuring that your lessons provide students with a variety of different types of stimulus from a variety of sources. English teachers, which texts have you chosen for KS3? Are they all written by dead white men? If so, consider texts from different writers. Want to re-engage students in food tech? Create dishes from different continents. Maths? Contextualise the problem in a real-life situation. Try some role play – it doesn't matter how you embed the experience, but giving students opportunities to essentially live out some of the ideas, feelings and experiences we so often tell them about gives them a considerably deeper understanding and allows them to build empathy. An example that won't leave my head, is when I was teaching poetry and some of the students couldn't conceptualise the way in which sand moves so freely because they'd never felt sand (an incredible thing considering the beach is ten miles from the school.) The solution was to go and buy a couple of bags of sand and dump it into mixing bowls from food tech and let them sift it, move it, blow it and try to make statues from it. The result? A springboard for me to access a poem that focuses around the shifting nature of humanity and power written in a desert setting. Before this, I was just saying words to them, but by enriching the experience, they were able to conceptualise something that before was theoretical to them.

### Language

Empowerment through language is a huge factor in building cultural capital. Without words, very little makes sense and a pivotal part of understanding the world is understanding the words used in the world, not only on the literal level but also the significance of implicatures and pragmatics. Rich discussion is paramount to a young person being able to interpret the world around them. Some children don't get much interaction outside of school (for a whole load of reasons – there's another book in that alone!) and for these children, the importance of interaction in school is amplified. Talking about ideas and feelings as well as emphasising and explicitly teaching how to interact in different contexts is something that is still hugely undervalued in the curriculum. The ability to talk effectively and in a way that allows an individual to express themselves is key to development and progression.

Taking the time to teach learners how, why and when to question is another way in which we can help them build their cultural capital. The skill of questioning, when modelled correctly, allows them to become more able to reflect on themselves and the world around them. Questioning their interpretations and their views often empowers them and gives them confidence. We are educating the voters of tomorrow, the thinkers of tomorrow and the leaders of tomorrow. Without the right skill set and the ability to question how, why and when, tomorrow will be a very different place. Making decisions is never easy, but if young people are well-equipped, we can but hope they make the right ones for themselves.

## Shared efficacy

Working collaboratively with others within your school allows you to build up understanding of the world and what it means to be a part of it through reinforcement of skills. Cultural capital has no subject boundaries; in fact, it is the glue that exists between each subject taught in schools. Making explicit links between learning is a sustainable way to encourage growth within your school. Cross-curricular links are a great way of building up both stronger understanding of topics and reducing workload. By working with other departments, you can ensure that you aren't doubling up on work. There are instances where the same context is taught in history, geography and English – think about how you can work with other departments to streamline your content and save effort and time.

Of course, there is still a whole curriculum to teach, let's not forget that. Building cultural capital shouldn't need to take away from curriculum time. In fact, to the contrary, it should enhance the experiences of students engaging with subject content. Consider, diversify and deliver. Take time to weave in opportunities to build cultural capital to ensure that you are preparing your learners for beyond the exams and you'll reduce your workload through them being more rounded, well-experienced learners.

- Do you embed wider learning into your lessons?
- How many opportunities do you give your students to broaden their cultural capital?
- Why might cultural capital be valuable in your subject?

- What does your school do to enrich students' experiences?
- How could you build the cultural capital of your students?

Taking some time to reflect on how effectively embedding experiences into your teaching may benefit students will change the way you think about the content of your lessons. Adjusting the experiences students have, be that in a tokenistic way or through more explicit means, will enrich their learning and in the long term this will have a huge impact on their take-home knowledge from you lessons. How does this link to workload? Well, if you teach them something that they are able to remember and engage with, it's more likely that they will conceptualise it more clearly – this in turn means that they should be more successful at retaining and reapplying the idea, saving you the difficulty of re-teaching abstract concepts.

# 3   Classroom space

When I think about classroom space, I always think back to my own experience of GCSE maths. I never really appreciated why Mr Ramm laid his classroom out in single desk rows (old ink pot holes still very present) and quietly played classical music in his office, just loud enough for us to hear. At the time I just thought that he was super-strict and didn't want us talking.

It wasn't until I left school that I actually realised it was all done on purpose. As a class, we were by far the best behaved in that room and overall (if there were such thing as progress figures then) we'd have all been significantly above where we should have been. Mr Ramm's seemingly random approach wasn't so random. It was simple and effective and it worked. It suited his subject and teaching style and it got results.

Anecdotes aside, there's a certain degree of psychology around space and how it's used. Your classroom is no different.

If you're lucky you'll have your own classroom; if not, I'd hope you'd still be teaching in a classroom in which the desks aren't fixed. Either way, how you use the space in which you teach is something you can simplify and manipulate to help streamline both your own delivery and the way in which the learners engage in the space in which you teach. I'm not saying you need to go full-on Mr Ramm here, but what I'm saying is, you might want to have a think about how your current set-up looks.

- Where do you have your desks?
- Why have you got them set up like this?
- Can you circulate around every seat?
- What displays do you have on the walls?
- What else do you have in your room?
- What kind of technology do you have at your disposal?

Before your students have even started working, you may be creating more work for yourself than you realise. Too often, we overlook the practicalities when it comes to teaching and we focus so much on what we are doing as practitioners – remember an actor can only perform if they have an appropriate stage. Get your room right and you might be able to avoid yourself some extra work in the long run.

## Classroom layout

When you walk into a classroom, you want to see that it's a good space for learning. Children are no different to us adults. If your space is cramped and cluttered, messy and disorganised, you're already sending a message to the students entering – even if it's unintentional. So where do we start when it comes to reducing your workload and making the most from your space?

We all sit and ponder our seating plans sometimes and think about how we could use them to solve specific problems or challenges, but not as often do we think about the physical features of our rooms. There is a lot of debate about the most advantageous way to organise your classroom and there are, of course, factors that are out of your control in some cases (like walls and pillars) but most learning spaces can be manipulated to be advantageous learning spaces and there are a number of things in any classroom that can be changed to make your life easier.

## The desks

One of the most important factors of classroom set up is where the desks are placed. Each set-up has distinct advantages and disadvantages and there is no system that is absolutely perfect.

It still amazes me that some teachers have taught for ten years without experimenting with their desk formats. After trying a number of different approaches, the irony is that for my teaching style and for my teaching groups I tend to go for rows. That's not to say I haven't tried and tested every combination going – you have to find what works for you and your space. My classroom is actually two cupboards with the wall knocked through, so my space is dictated to me. The narrow nature of my classroom affords me little other option, as for me circulation is key. I've even done away with my desk (because I never use it.)

What are the alternatives to rows though? Below are some of the approaches to seating set-ups that provide distinct advantages over the traditional row format. Depending on your group, your subject and your space, you might be able to put these to the test. Before you decide on which seating plan works for you, consider:

- Exactly what you need from your classroom.
- Do you need to circulate?
- Do you use a lot of collaborative talk?
- Does your subject suit a lecture style?
- Can you classes cope with the additional extraneous load that may come with vision of others?
- What kind of an environment are you trying to create?

### Two by Two

- Pros: Easy group work, free movement for teacher, good presence and visibility at the front of class.
- Cons: Pupils can distract each other, limited visual access to displays, no space for tutorial time.

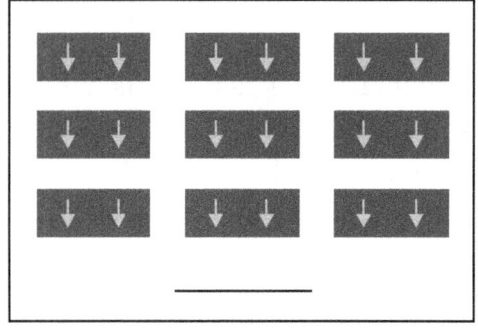 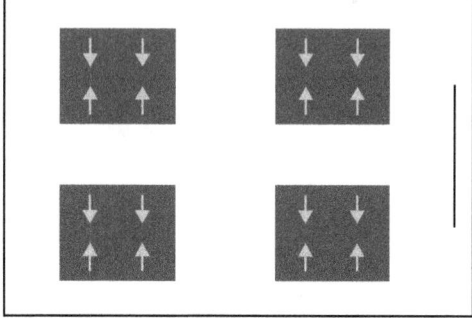

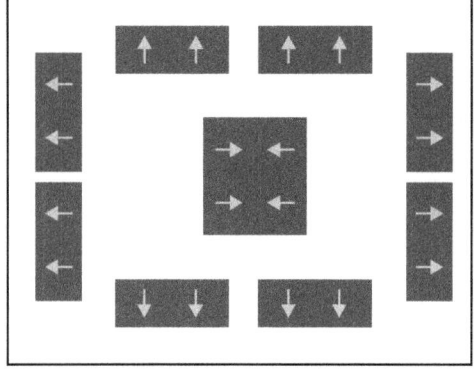 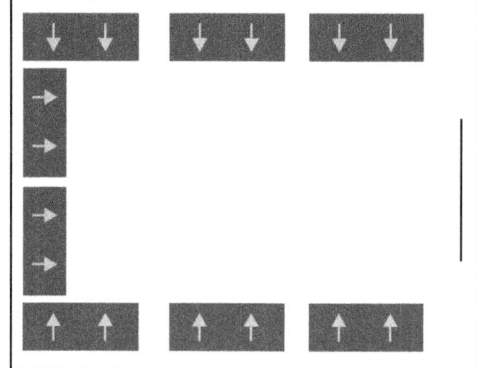

### The Island

- Pros: Excellent tutorial space, central point of contact, safe for pupils to question.
- Cons: Not constant visual contact with teacher, more difficulty with group work, pupils need to move a lot.

### Four by Four

- Pros: Effective differentiation, group tasks take no rearranging, easy support and access.
- Cons: Spacing can be an issue in smaller classrooms.

### The Horseshoe

- Pros: Open forum for questioning and lecturing, everyone engages with each other, teacher can reach everyone.
- Cons: Possible distractions, group work can be a difficulty.

Remember that in most classrooms the desks aren't fixed, so you have room to try a number of different approaches before you find your favoured seating approach. Taking into account the diversity of pupils you are likely to teach, experimenting with the layout of the room can be an effective way of managing behaviour and can help to boost engagement. You don't want it to turn into musical tables at the end of each lesson, but sometimes setting the desks up differently can allow a different dynamic in the lesson. In addition, the concept of change is something that is likely to build resilience in learners' minds.

If you teach a class that requires group or individual tutorial time, the Island layout allows the teacher to bring pupils to the centre of the room while the others in the class continue with work. Because they are facing away from the rest of the class, distraction is minimised. In addition, the teacher can oversee them while engaging in a tutorial with the selected members of the class – although possible, this kind of interaction is simply a pain in a normal row format.

In complete contrast, if you are teaching a discussion-based subject, a Horseshoe layout gives distinct advantages. The pupils are able to interact with every other member of the class, the teacher can circulate with ease and pupils have a good view of the whole room while working. The horseshoe can also be modified to have rows in the middle to allow for full circulation and further reduction of distraction. This approach is really good for classrooms that lack space to accommodate a full horseshoe.

Getting the seats in the right place might seem simple but it can have a huge impact on the dynamic of your room; after all, the likeness is that the students will be in those seats while you're teaching them for hours and hours over a year.

## The pupils

Once you've got the seats in the right place you need to think about how you're going to fill them. Where you sit your proverbial customers is the other major factor in class dynamic, and getting it wrong can create a whole host of issues that could potentially increase your workload.

Is there a winning formula? It's difficult to get it right, that's for sure. There are approaches you can adopt and things you can remember to ensure you don't fall into the common early career pitfalls when it comes to seating plans.

The first big thing is overcomplicating the puzzle. Whatever you do, you're likely to encounter some level of resistance at some point in the year. Spending hours on seating plans is one of those things that drastically increases workload. My advice as always is to keep it simple but with a few key points in mind.

Boy-girl-boy-girl? No. Well yes, but it is not quite as simple as that. And what's more, it does not need to be as consistent as that (assuming your school doesn't have a policy that demands it). Remember, there is little evidence to suggest the effects of grouping by ability within lessons, it actually makes very little difference to learning outcomes (Higgins et al., 2013). Instead, focus your student seating on factors other than similar abilities.

We have all observed the teacher who sits the naughtiest boy next to the nicest girl – don't do it. Let's take one of the classroom four set-up examples we have illustrated: Four by Four. The distribution of (a hypothetical but typical class) may go like this…

Think about the needs of the pupils when you think of seating them. For example, for those with fragile confidence or other social anxiety issues, place them as near to the door as possible and leave the door open. This will subtly manage their fight or flight feelings by allowing them, subconsciously, to have an "out" and not to feel trapped or boxed in.

For pupils with ADHD or similar then the standard teacher response is to isolate them, usually at the "front" of a class virtually facing a wall to keep them away from distractions. It rarely works (cue wriggling in seat, etc.). Why not sit them at the desk with the liveliest view? This is usually in the middle of the room when you cluster your tables in groups of four or six pupils. This helps address their need for distraction, and actually can help them focus better in the lesson.

Shy or quiet pupils? Seat them together and make sure you access them regularly. Really low-ability boy? Then sit him with three of the brightest girls, with his back to his mates or on the opposite side of the room. The girls will help the boy, and also he will have limited opportunities to get involved with his friends in the class.

It may seem rudimentary but it's sometimes what is needed. The rule is, as always, know your class and I mean really know them. Along with that, make sure they know your expectations for behaviour and most importantly for learning. The seating plan should be well considered, but in honesty, anyone should be able to sit anywhere and get on... as long as you make that clear. Yes, as an early career teacher it's not always the reality, so in the short term, rig your seating plan up in a way that helps you.

## The displays

Displays are time holes and if they aren't thought through, they can actually detract from learning. Too many classrooms only have displays on boards made of ply, neatly decorated with sugar paper, a frilly border and the work of pupils from three years before. Bin it. It isn't helping anyone. Fisher et al. (2014) found that students are less likely to stay focused in a highly decorated classroom and that students who were taught in this kind of environment got lower test scores than those taught in a more sparsely decorated room.

Displays need to be useful. They need to help the learning of the pupil – but how?

The first thing to have focal points. That means simply don't plaster your walls with random words, hang things from the ceiling and generally make the room look like a maze of paper. Make your room a 360-degree experience, but group resources together. Key terms in one place, writing frames in another and exemplars in another. Keep the cognitive load low by guiding students around the displays. Make them a resource that you refer to in your teaching and keep referring to them – this makes them memorable. Use your room to guide your kids through their exam; key words/vocabulary, phrases, concepts, graphs, pictures, models of work with annotations.

Don't just have your displays as static resources, however; it's a waste. Remove terms and resources and use the gaps for recall exercises. Build in low-stakes testing around your displays and most of all replicate them (if you can) so that students can use them at home. What's better than having the classroom with you when you aren't there? Little tricks like this are a great way to build engagement with resources that take you time to make. Anything you can do to get more mileage and usage out of the things you've ploughed time into, the more valuable those resources become.

Plan out your space and decide what you are going to have on each surface. Yes surface. Don't stick to just the walls! Ceilings (with care!), windows and desks are all fair game for some kind of learning display. Will you ever stop little Jimmy gazing out of the window during period 4 on a Friday? No? Okay, write ten keywords on that window and at least try to give him something of relevance to look at! Again exercise with caution, you don't want it to be a circus, but if it's clear and usable it may help learning.

And not only will it improve the learning experience of your pupils, a good display will improve your teaching experience. Displays that model work or a paragraph structure, for example, save reams of time and frustration. Just imagine not having to repeat concepts that have been covered (sometimes many, many times) before! A reference point allows you to reduce your workload when you are in the classroom by having a point to which you can reference – this is really helpful with key terms and phrasing, "How do I say..." can be remedied with point in the right direction. You only have to do this a couple of times before the resource has paid for itself (so to speak) and the student's study habits improve as a result.

Of course displays can come at a price – financially and time-wise. Spread the load between members of the department for a shared approach. The concept of shared efficacy is more powerful than any other classroom tool and having consistency across a department makes the resource considerably more impactful.

Some teachers like to have their own touches in a classroom. Each to their own, but to my mind, a classroom is my place of business and I like things kept tight. Again, consider what kind of an environment you're trying to foster. Trinkets and lucky charms aside, make sure that you consider cognitive load and make your displays centred around learning.

## Desk or no desk?

A typical classroom has a number of pieces of furniture in it beside the student's desks. Be it a cupboard or some random desks that are just there – well because they are – you need to question if you need them. Even your desk. Do you need it?

In most classrooms, the teacher has a desk. Although most do not have the stereotypical apple placed on the corner from an endearing student, teacher's desks are a typical part of any classroom scene – but should they be used during lessons?

There are certain practicalities that a desk affords – a place for your computer, somewhere you to put your coffee (in a sealed cup, of course) and a dumping ground for any extra hand-outs that you copy and have no other home for.

Besides these practicalities, I would argue that your desk should not be used during lesson time. It may be controversial to say it, but teachers should not be sat behind their desks.

I work with a lot of trainee teachers and they use the desk at the front of the class in a novel way. It is used as a kind of barricade between themselves and the class – it provides them with a physical wooden barrier that they often feel (initially at least) gives them some protection from the rabid horde in front of them.

Of course, they quickly come to realise that standing behind their desk inhibits them from truly dominating the front of the classroom, and as their confidence grows, they venture out from their safe place into the realms of the unknown.

I can understand why trainees naturally take this approach – the classroom can be a scary place after all, but experienced teachers (more often than not) do not use their desk as a barrier, they use it to do "nothing".

Can you honestly say that you know what is happening on the other side of your classroom from behind your desk? By "what is happening" I mean, for example, what (exactly) is being written in a book during a task.

So many teachers have fallen into the habit of starting a task and letting their class get on with it. It is understandable – the class look engaged, they have started well, there are no questions, you have got five emails to send from yesterday and the time would be wasted if you watched the class work – but it is wrong (well right, but wrong). Being active during tasks is a really effective way to keep on top of misconceptions, support learning and most importantly (for me) reduce my workload outside of the classroom.

Keep it simple and ask yourself these questions… and answer honestly because I'm not saying get rid of your desk if you actually need it:

- Why do you have a desk in your room?

- What do you use your desk for?

- How much time do you spend at it or behind it each lesson?

- Do you use it out of lessons?

## Clutter

Keep your room clutter-free. A clutter-free space means a clutter-free mind. If you have surfaces you don't use, get rid of them. Spare desks and random cupboards with the doors falling off need to go. Thaler and Sunstein (2010) highlight that seemingly insignificant factors can have a massive impact on behaviours, and for me clutter is one of the elements that fall within this bracket. Don't leave dictionaries and workbooks on the windowsills and try to keep your space as clean as you can. I know it's hard, but once again it comes down to expectations. If you treat your room like a tip, the kids will too and it'll only exacerbate your stress.

Much like your displays, keep everything in order and only keep hold of it if it serves a function. Think about the feng shui. Can you get around the obstacles? Can the kids get round the obstacles? Is that desk at the front why every lesson starts with distraction (because little Billy insists on tripping over it, much to his cronies' delight)? Thom (2018) quite rightly states that "we may glow with joy as we look around our new sparse classroom walls and shelves and allow ourselves some internal massaging [...] but] sustaining this new minimalist habit is challenging". There's no doubt that a clear-out is refreshing, but for decluttering to truly impact your workload, it must be sustained. Don't let the standard slip, as clawing it back can be hard work.

Linking workload to a messy classroom might not be what you were expecting, but it all factors in and when you think about it, minimising distraction and confusion are ways to make learning more efficient. Davenport and Scott (2015) highlight that unnecessary "stuff" can cause a lot of negative feelings – we want our classrooms to be safe learning spaces, and minimising the impact of unnecessary elements can reduce the stress of both teachers and students, leading to less anxiety and more productivity.

- Have you got anything that you don't need in your classroom?
- Is there any furniture that is obsolete or serving no function?
- Can you get rid of anything that is old and replace it?
- Do you need to store what you do in your classroom? Are there alternatives?

## Why is it so important to consider your space?

Now we've talked about shifting your classroom around and getting everything just so, let's think about what you can now do with it. One common misconception and an equally common pitfall for a lot of new teachers is that they need to be front and centre in the classroom. If you have the correct space, you can exploit this in a number of ways.

### Circulating

The concept of walking around your classroom is not something new. Good circulation means that you can keep your students engaged in tasks, support them when they are stuck and stretch them as they work. With a well laid-out room, circulation becomes a lot easier and also your circulation becomes more inclusive.

Your movement round the classroom needs to be calculated. Simply floating from desk to desk is not always enough to ensure that you are supporting the learning as well as you could be. Having the right layout and space means that you can plan your routes to assist students depending on the task they are completing.

If your classes are anything like mine, you often have a huge variety of needs in one room. For example, I know that certain students in my classes struggle more with longer writing tasks, whereas comprehension is an issue for other children. By building your space correctly, you can address arising need effectively by having access to all students.

As such, having set routes gives additional value to your seating plan and you can pre-plan where and how you are going to support individuals depending on the tasks being set. This opens a whole additional avenue when it comes to pre-planning misconceptions that may arise, something we will explore later.

And it is not just a matter of knowing where you are going, it is also important that you consider your behaviour as you circulate. Be mindful of the space between you and the pupil to whom you are speaking or those you are keen to observe. In a cramped environment, discussion becomes more pressured and there is the risk that students feel entrapped. The last thing you want to be is intimidating, so you need to ensure that your students embrace your circulating and checking by showing them how powerful this kind of support can be.

## Tracking, not watching

An improved layout means that you are able to begin to refine your practice too. Doug Lemov (2015) conceptualises the idea of tracking not watching perfectly – the idea simply is that one of the most important skills for any teacher or coach is observing during independent practice.

Observing is not watching – observing means looking at practice and calculating your next actions. While a teacher circulates the class they need to make a note (mentally or physically) of what needs addressing or readdressing in order for the class to improve. By effectively tracking misconceptions and successes, teaching becomes responsive and learning is more efficient. With the right set-up, this activity is something that can reduce workload outside the classroom significantly, as misconceptions can be picked up, recorded or addressed immediately. Observing live learning means that you can reduce the time you might normally spend trawling through books in a de-contextualised environment; moreover, the students get the live input that helps them overcome any issues they encounter there and then.

Of course, for this kind of an approach to be effective, you need to be flexible and reflective in your planning – but by addressing misconceptions as they arise, teachers can make much better use of their lesson time.

An additional advantage of tracking your class as they learn is that you are able to actively intervene while they are working in the moment. This encourages them to stay engaged but it also adds a personalised element to your teaching and can stop misconceptions becoming embedded.

You become less of a distant figure at the front of the class and you show students that you value each individual's learning and progress. When you are considering classroom layout, factor in how empowering it can be for you as the teacher to have free roam of the room.

This can lead to a significant increase in motivation for learning and it also builds a culture of trust. As we all know, students are notoriously reluctant to show their misunderstandings in front of their peers, so by effectively tracking their misconceptions and successes, and intervening as your circulate, we are able to take some of the threat (and guesswork) out of the learning process.

Another massive bonus is the heightened engagement you can foster through tracking. Students stay on topic more because they are more supported and, in turn, learning is significantly more effective.

## Marking

The space to manoeuvre doesn't just mean that you can help students with their work. It means that you can get involved yourself. I do not mark books outside the classroom. I have not done this for a while now. Effective circulation and tracking means that I can achieve two things that remove the need for any out-of-class marking: whole-class feedback and live marking. We'll discuss these in depth later in the book, but the freedom of movement that comes about from decluttering means that you can work more efficiently.

The most effective time to get feedback is while you are still doing something. Think about how effective it is being redirected as and when you are doing something wrong. Now imagine you are going wrong and somebody takes a day or a week to intervene and set you right again – it is frustrating. Having the right working space means that you can get involved while the students are working.

One of the reasons I got rid of my desk was because I've seen so many teachers over the years barricaded behind the desk or being tempted to send the odd email while the class are working. I would much prefer to do my marking in class and send my emails later than the other way around... again, it comes down to prioritising – I'd much prefer to send an email outside of school time if I need to than to take 30 books home with me.

Effective in-class marking means you can instantly improve the outcomes of a task, but you also build the students' confidence and their skills by highlighting shortcomings in their responses immediately. You are modelling how they can question their own work, building again that factor of self-efficacy.

Making use of your time by circulating and reading is such a powerful way of gauging the progress of your class and it allows you to know where the shortcomings are in real time, not two days later.

### Reality

There is no classroom in the world where at least some change in layout would not improve the learning environment. The above is not an exhaustive list of ideas, but hopefully it gets you thinking about what might work for you and your own class. You can't move walls (well, I had to in my case) and you are sometimes constrained by institutional policies and regulations, but do what you can with what you have.

Think your space through, remove any thing that doesn't have a function or contribute in any way and then make the most of your space. I never asked Mr Ramm, but that's totally the advice he'd give.

- How are you going to maximise the impact of your classroom layout?
- Can you justify how these changes will help your teaching?
- What will you do with your displays this year?
- Are there any items in your room that you will get rid of now?
- How can your classroom space save you time outside of lessons?

# 4 Planning

Planning a lesson may mean a number of different things to different teachers. For me the word *planning* has extremely negative connotations; it brings back memories of having to do those long lesson pro formas before every lesson on my PGCE, just for them to be filed (in a poly wallet, printed double-sided) and never to be seen again. The thought of the hours I spent on those makes me shudder, as does the fact that some schools still think that external observers want to see a lesson plan every time they walk into a lesson (they don't, just to clarify).

Lesson planning in this rigid and structured format has its place during training, as consideration of the elements of a lesson are really important, as are the expected outcomes. But for experienced teachers, planning should be a lot more simple and hopefully less time-consuming. But what and who are you currently planning for?

- How do you plan for the activities in your lessons?
- What do you actually plan for?
- Who are you planning for?
- How long is your lesson planning taking?
- Do you use your plan?

Now, I'm not going to give you some amazing way to never have to plan again, I'm sorry, I haven't figured that out yet. There are, however, a number of different approaches that you can adopt for yourself and as a collective in your department to reduce the workload around planning.

There are a number of approaches to planning that we could discuss, but honestly, I wouldn't be able to tell you much more than you already know about long-, short- and medium-term planning – I won't insult your intelligence by defining each. Instead, let's think about how we can factor good teaching into our planning that is focused around skills… because let's face it, students don't just start doing things by magic.

## What to plan

You need to plan your lessons, that's a given – how you plan them and what you plan for is the key to saving time and stress. Throughout training and into your career as a teacher, planning and preparation will inevitably take up a chunk of your time. As education moves away from micro-management of individual minutes in lessons (hopefully), some of this pressure is relieved. But with a legacy of having "the lesson plan" handy, and years of being told that each phase of learning needs to be accounted for, some teachers still feel the burden. Re-evaluating what exactly you are planning can be a real time-saver and it can hugely reduce your workload.

Traditionally, lessons have always been seen to have three main parts (starters, mains and plenaries). When thinking about planning a lesson, don't assume they need to have these three parts. Also, forget about constant mini-plenaries and other fads that have come and gone. Think logically and make sure that you include the right ingredients that help understanding and build knowledge. This will in turn allow you to build a kind of lesson formula that ensures that you focus on the learning and not on what the learning looks like. Rosenshine's principles of instruction are all you need for this. Modelling, scaffolding, independent practice, periodical review are all phases that you need to consider including… but knowing that you're going to use these in one guise or another means that you have a backbone on which you can build. The principles are by no means a checklist, I repeat, *not a checklist*, but they certainly allow you to consider carefully how you can ensure learning is structured, sequential and, most importantly, supported at all points. Also, factoring in phases to check for understanding allows you to ascertain when learning has actually taken place. A mistake that the legacy of three-part planning has left is that learning has only happened at the end of a phase or in fact at the end of a lesson; we know this isn't the case.

Variety will always remain the spice of life, but don't feel you need something new and whizzy every lesson. In fact, sometimes it's better to go old-school and get instructivist. Enthusiasm for "discovery learning" is not supported by research evidence (Kirschner et al., 2006). Although learners do need to build new understanding on what they already know, if teachers want them to learn new ideas, knowledge or methods they need to teach them directly, and this correlates with the concept that planning needs to focus around tangible teaching. There are topics and times where you will need to be creative with the ways in which you teach content, but think about how much value you get from the time you put in. Consider the additional resources you need for lessons and keep them to a minimum.

Planning doesn't just include your time sat thinking about the lesson, it also includes the time you spend making diagrams, printing hand-outs and generally getting things ready. Box clever and minimise unnecessary frills. Ask yourself: what impact is this going to have on the learning? If the answer is *not a lot*, simplify it. The time you save can be used in so many better ways. Please, please, please don't spend time creating individual resources for students in your classes and think that it shows "differentiation". This is a trap that not only creates the wrong type of learning environment (and message), it also takes up a huge amount of teacher time. The psychological evidence shows that there are no benefits for learning from trying to present information to learners in their preferred learning style (Willingham 2008) so practice like this is simply pointless. Support for learners should come through scaffolding, modelling and teacher input, not from "the easier worksheet"... just don't do it! The same goes for anything about learning styles and resources. It's not a thing. Stick to quality teaching, you're the expert.

Learning needs to be structured, but you also need to be flexible and able to react to student misconceptions as they inevitably arise. Over-planning can lead to time being wasted on phases and resources that aren't used or, worse, rigidity that means misconceptions aren't addressed. To make sure that you save yourself time in the long run, plan opportunities for you to be reactive to the learning that is taking place. Do away with pro formas that nobody looks at, forget about the word differentiation and don't create reams of worksheets where a simple slide will suffice. Reducing your planning workload will have a huge impact on the quality of your actual teaching.

## Talking

If we were to ask pupils about the most daunting tasks in school, among them would be speaking in lessons. If we were to ask teachers what is one of the most under-planned phases of their lessons was, I'd say the phases around student talk. The reason is that often teachers neglect to teach students how to speak because they neglect to plan for it. The focus on oracy is growing and it is an area that a lot of teachers are now looking to build on in their practice.

For the quieter members of your class, the idea of speaking sparks anxiety and fear and even the most confident pupil can worry about putting their heads above the proverbial parapet when it comes to class discussions. The problem with this is that pupils need to learn how to speak, discuss and debate, not least because classroom talk is such a powerful way of learning. So how can we as teachers encourage pupils to speak more and with confidence?

It's certainly no easy task and ensuring that our expectations are clear around talk is one of the cornerstones of success.

I cast my mind back to my first lesson in front of a class as a teacher and I vividly remember asking my class to "talk" about Tommo and Charlie's relationship in *Private Peaceful* – a great book. My delight when they started talking was palpable, I was so proud of myself... until about 20 seconds in, when the class started going wildly off topic and it all fell apart. That was a while ago, but the memory always remind me of the dangers of being vague with expectations when I set spoken tasks.

Talking needs to be defined and clear for it to have a purpose; if it has no purpose, it loses value. If talk loses value, students become lethargic and disengaged with talking and you lose one of your tools for classroom variation.

On the most simple level, speaking in the classroom, to my mind, has two main categories – discussion talk and presentational talk. Teachers often switch their expectations of students when it comes to talk very quickly and with very little regard for how much a cognitive challenge this is.

On the one hand, discussion is a collaborative type of talk which allows students to share ideas. Talking to your partner or to peers in a small group can be a huge confidence builder, especially if a task is set up in a way that gives clear discussion points. Conversely, presentational talk is significantly more formal and requires a different set of skills, namely the ability to vocalise and summarise your ideas in an eloquent manner.

We can help students with this by teaching them about how to discuss and how to present. By making the difference between the two types of talk explicit, we are able to build confidence in talking by ensuring that students are fully aware of the expectations of each type of talk. By setting out the parameters and using a common language, you can quickly make it very clear to learners what your expectations are around talk and, in turn, make the process less extraneous.

A key feature of any discussion in class is specific key terms. These differ from subject to subject (of course) but they are an essential part of building confidence in pupils. The best way to integrate these is to have rich discussions around ideas. Building in high expectations around terminology is paramount to student success with regard to assimilation of these terms.

As the teacher, you need to model the use of these key terms so that the pupils can see them being used in context. Have them on display to act as discussion prompts and starters.

Encouraging students to become more independent around their discovery of words is another way in which you can encourage talk. Giving students the responsibility of working with the words will in turn increase their ownership of such vocabulary. By shifting the expectation away from you, you are able to build a culture of self-efficacy.

In addition, teaching them about the significance of word families, suffixes and prefixes will help them to build their knowledge and then use that knowledge to get to grips with unfamiliar words. This boosts confidence and further reduces the barriers that are built from the fear of failure.

Finally, consider which words you need to focus on; an overload of vocabulary can be counterproductive, especially when it comes to speaking. Make sure you have a regular key word spot in your lessons, as repeat exposure to words builds up familiarity, which in turn adds to pupils' confidence. Avoiding timely exercises that focus on teaching vocabulary out of context will reduce your workload significantly.

Linking talking and writing is something that needs to be explicit. Pupils often miss the intrinsic relationship between the two and see them as two disassociated skills. Talking came first, writing came afterwards – writing is a by-product of speaking.

Try changing the expectation in your classroom so that pupils have to verbalise answers in full sentences just as they would write them. Discussion frames are simply writing frames refocused. Not only will this improve your class discussions, it will also have a huge impact on the quality of your pupils' written work. Getting students into good habits with speaking isn't a time-consuming process; again, it comes down to scaffolding and modelling. Modelling good discussion can be achieved with simple guidance and through effective habits of discussion. It is easy to forget that we are discussing all of the time in class and quite often we overlook the importance of ensuring that the talk is effective and efficient.

An example might be a task that involves persuasion or argument. The first hurdle for some learners is that they do not know (or cannot remember) how to modify their talk to fit this purpose.

With some talking frames in the shape of phrases or sentence starters, the discussion they have with their peers, or that you have as a whole class, becomes significantly more valuable and as a teacher, modelling how to use these approaches further assists your class.

It follows that an improvement in speaking should translate to an improvement in writing due to the cognitive overlap in terms of thinking (not application) of the two skills.

Careful, this is much more complicated than it sounds. The most important thing to remember is that if a pupil does not want to talk, any threat in any form will be used as an excuse for not doing so. A safe environment contains no threats, and that is what as teachers we must aim for. Having clear expectations of pupils is the first step – making sure that everyone is treated equally and fairly is a given, but ensuring there is mutual respect for all speakers as well as empathy really adds to the confidence of the shyest pupils. Simply knowing that they will not be ridiculed is something that empowers them.

Another way in which you can reduce threat is by ensuring that you are consistent and transparent with your approach to talk in the classroom. Following certain methods of questioning in each lesson makes students feel comfortable with responding. Things you can think about include how you approach questioning – cold call, hands up, will the pupils have time to prepare to talk, can you pre-warn pupils that they will be contributing?

It is incredible how responsive students can be if they are aware of a teacher's approach. And it is equally startling how mute they can go if they are not! If the class knows the expectations, then they know where the goalposts are – we should not be trying to catch them out when we get them to talk.

Always look at creating opportunities for small-scale discussion between a few pupils as well as group and whole-class activities and make sure these are planned in. So much of our planned time is dedicated to writing, but we must not neglect planning for talk.

Start small and work your way up – do not try to get everyone involved in whole-class discussions at first, but aim to have everyone contribute by the end of the term or scheme of work.

Creating a non-threatening environment will encourage the members of your class to feel more comfortable with the prospect of speaking. It sounds simple but it is one of the cornerstones for a successful talking classroom.

- How can you plan for talk?
- How can you use talk more effectively in your lessons?
- What will your expectations be around talk?
- How will you make your students aware of your expectations?
- How will you measure the success?

## Modelling

Planning needs to always take into account the end game. Ensuring that your students know what to aim for is an important factor in their learning journey and in their understanding of an idea. Providing models isn't just good teaching practice, it's common sense. If you think about flat-pack furniture, it always has a picture of the end product on the front, before the instructions begin. Teaching should be no different. Making the expectation of outcome clear at the start deals with misconceptions that may arise through disambiguation. Of course, some will challenge this idea and say that this reduces the level of challenge… but of course it doesn't if it's set up properly. Modelling your expectations streamlines your teaching and helps you to be significantly more effective with your time and the time of the students, and for this you need to be well prepared.

Measured failure and desirable difficulty are also key parts of learning, but making sure that the difficulty and failure come at the right time is key. By modelling your expectations for tasks, you are able to make sure that your teaching has the right levels of success and challenge. Efficient modelling can also drastically reduce your workload outside of the classroom.

In the most simple form, modelling is about seeing before doing and therefore minimising the ambiguity around an outcome. It follows that learning and the application of learning is then streamlined and students are able to effectively mould their own practice around the teacher's examples. Forwarding the expectation means that students are completely clear with what is expected of them from the outset, meaning that time, energy and brain power isn't wasted on doing a task wrong and it saves misconceptions and errors from arising.

It is, of course, a bit more complex than this in practice, especially as subjects vary so much in terms of content and outcomes. However, there are some simple ways to ensure effective modelling.

There is nothing more empowering for a class than seeing their teacher do what is expected of them (and do it really, really well). Live modelling allows students to see how an answer can be formulated. That correlation between thought process and articulation of ideas on paper is often a step that teachers miss – but it is such a powerful tool. Live modelling allows students to see how to formulate a paragraph, an argument or a response. It also allows teachers to question students and get their input. Of course, you have to be confident in your subject knowledge to succeed with this approach – you need to be able to practise what you preach.

Using a structure as simple as *I do, we do, you do* gives students the feeling of security in that they have first seen what is expected of them as you change the stimulus and remove the support, you are then able to increase the desirable difficulty and start your process of checking for understanding.

Modelling is all about providing a target for students to aspire to. The model you provide needs to be of sufficient quality and so being clear on what the success criteria are is of paramount importance (teaching topics can be tough enough without creating misconceptions from substandard modelling). For exam groups, it is always good practice to use exam board exemplars to inform your modelling to ensure that you do not model the wrong thing. At Key Stage 3, modelling should follow similar criteria to that in Key Stage 4 – the way in which the information is presented will, of course, be very different, but the end goal remains the same. Ultimately, consistency in approach is key.

Regardless of what you are teaching, misconceptions will arise. Making sure that your modelling is planned to "pre-address" common misconceptions means that you do not waste valuable teaching time and that students remain engaged and motivated. Doug Lemov's tracking model is one way misconceptions can be tracked live within lessons, and his principles for planning for misconceptions during curriculum design are an equally powerful tool (see Lemov, 2015).

Modelling is an effective way of avoiding misconceptions altogether. By highlighting common stumbling blocks, you can prepare your lessons and sequences of learning accordingly. A lot of confusion in learning comes during the application and well-planned and well-timed examples are an effective way of circumnavigating issues – if you see them coming. If you cannot see them and they arise, you can then use live modelling to clear up misunderstandings.

One of the biggest misconceptions from teachers when it comes to modelling is that it is removing the challenge from tasks if you show the students the outcomes you want. I vehemently contest that.

When I do training on modelling, I often use the analogy of drawing a tree. My instruction is to draw a tree: one person draws a palm tree, one draws an oak, and two draw a tree with no branches. Now I have a problem – all have followed the instruction, but what kind of tree was I expecting? Without a clear model of expectation, how is a student going to do exactly what you want of them?

Of course there are times when you model the intentional opposite; it is not all about showing students exactly what to do, but also what not to do.

Modelling bad responses is also a good way of allowing students to engage with common errors. By highlighting what not to do, teachers are able to teach students what to look out for in their own work. In my subject, English, my favourite is starting creative writing with "The...". Pupils are in absolute uproar if I ever start any writing with this determiner because it is something they have been conditioned to avoid.

Modelling is about showing and applying. One big mistake that teachers often make is that they do not allow students to apply the learning from the model in a suitable context. It is futile to give a model and then getting students to simply apply it (perhaps having changed only minor details) – they will just copy blindly. Instead, the stimulus, the input, the quote or the source need to be substituted so that pupils have an opportunity to apply the modelled ideas in a separate and different task.

Removing the scaffolding is something that increases the desirable difficulty and moves tasks much more toward the level of challenge that we know is so necessary for learning. Remember, if we do not increase the level of challenge, we are not effectively modelling.

Effective modelling makes you a better teacher. Models are enablers – they are there to help students see what outcomes could/should look like. Modelling allows your students to engage and succeed and it reduces your workload because common misconceptions are addressed as or before they arise

- Are you currently modelling your expectations of writing?
- Do you make it clear what your expectations are of writing?
- Can you practice what you are preaching?

## Being responsive – the art of winging it

In life, there are situations where you just need to go with the flow. No level of planning and consideration can possibly prepare you for the reality of what is to come. Teaching is a bit like that. You can spend hours and hours preparing the perfect lesson and it can go to pot in the first few minutes if you can't make that lesson fit the children in front of you. Don't be afraid to deviate from the plan. In fact I'd go as far as to say the best lessons I have seen in my (many, many) observations are the ones where the teacher has a goal, but exhibits the skills to be able to manipulate their plan to accommodate for the learners in front of them.

Think about these questions and try to answer them truthfully:

- How comfortable are you going off-piste with learning?
- Have you ever felt out of control in a lesson?
- Do you know when it's a good idea to move away from what you planned?
- How do you measure success in your lessons?

Are you ever really winging it?

I talk whimsically about winging it, but in truth, any exceptional teacher never really wings it completely. You must go into every lesson with a good idea of what you want the outcome to be for the students, be that in terms of knowledge, understanding or skills. Without a goal, lessons can become little more than a blob of discussion. I don't want to get into the complexities of lesson objectives, but without at least an idea of outcome, as a professional, it is difficult to measure your success and the progress of the students you are teaching.

On top of the goals or outcomes, you're likely to have some stimulus and hopefully some kind of plan of action as to how you'll use that stimulus. I tend to stay pretty simple and I prepare say 5–8 slides with minimal content to ensure that I have learning anchors and that I vary the tasks and difficulty of the learning in the lesson. I like to start with a recall phase (this week, last week, last month) and I always end with an application of some description. What happens in the middle often depends on how the students respond to the stimulus. You just never know which pieces of information students will run with and what kinds of discussions may arise.

Winging it isn't about turning up with a board pen and hoping for the best, that's laziness and regardless of how "old school" you may think it looks, not being planned is not cool. Winging it is about having the confidence to go with the learning and having a repertoire of skills required to keep students motivated and engaged when the planned activities and support just don't cut it.

Remembering that you will be winging it at times means that you begin to accept that some of the detailed planning that is taking you so long may not need doing in the way that you are doing it. As your confidence grows, your prompts will reduce and soon you'll have sparsely populated slides, not just because you understand about CLT, but because you don't need them. Over-planning is an addiction that often results in no increase in student attainment. I'm not saying that because I've done an in-depth study into it with the word "metacognition" in the title, I'm saying it because it's common sense and it's true. Come away from seeking solace in detail; if you can, stick to the ratio of one minute of your time costing the students ten minutes of theirs – it's a good ratio to have. If you're spending six minutes planning, they should have worked for an hour. You don't want it the other way round (please don't make card sorts!).

## Sharing the load

I sincerely hope that you are in a school that is already doing this, and if you're not then please try to persuade the powers that be to allow you to do this. Planning collaboratively is an obviously huge factor that reduces workload, but it is still a practice that is ineffectively utilised.

Shared teacher efficacy is one of the highest impacting factors on student outcomes (Hattie & Timperley, 2007). The collective vision and drive of a team has nearly twice the impact of effective feedback and triple the impact of study skills. It's absolutely phenomenal how powerful a team pulling in the same direction can be.

Gone are the days of focusing on personal progress and individual planning. I can't for the life of me understand leaders who allow 15 English teachers to individually plan and prepare separately for their classes – it makes no sense at all and the time cost is insane. Well thought through collaborative planning can massively cut down on the time teachers spend writing lessons and creating PowerPoints, and it allows teams to play to their strengths.

Collaborative planning is an excellent way to reduce the burden of teacher preparation. Having centralised schemes of learning allow consistency across a department and they also stop the wheel being reinvented three, four or even ten times over. Lessons will still require individual tweaking and personalising, but by working collectively and planning as a team, preparation becomes a significantly less laborious process. It's not just in school you can do this, however. Communities on Twitter are especially valuable to those who work in, let's say, less collegial contexts. Networking can be a huge time-saver, especially if you find like-minded individuals.

There should be a level of individualism about very lesson, there's no debate there, but by creating central resources, teachers are then able to work from a basis and not have to start from scratch. If you as a department or team embed exceptional pedagogy from the outset, the lessons will be pre-populated with incredibleness, all individuals will need to do is to make the lessons fit their classes… and that is a lot less work that doing every lesson alone.

Collaborative planning also opens the door for a number of CPD opportunities. By contributing to a scheme of work or series of lessons, you are able to flaunt your skills or to build your skills up. Working collaboratively allows teachers to help one another build their knowledge from each other. Quite often, I use planning to help individuals improve their knowledge of a topic by working with someone who knows it well. This boost confidence in teaching the unit and it also builds a sense of trust and professionalism.

What's more, collaborative planning frees up time for you to refine your practice. You focus less on providing the obvious building blocks for the learners in front of you and put your energies into ensuring that the learning is tailored for them. Again, the pitfall of this approach is simply that teachers try to teach a lesson (as is) to any group without the consideration of how the lesson should be modified, but again it comes down to expectations and good leadership

### Reality

You are the master of your own destiny when it comes to planning. My advice quite simply is to ensure that you are adequately prepared to teach the material that is required of you and that you also plan so the students are prepared to be able to respond to what you have planned. To get the most out of your time spent planning, you need to plan effectively by not overdoing it. If you can, share the load between teachers around you.

- Can you focus your planning more effectively now?
- Which factors can you cut out?
- Is there scope for collaborative planning in your department?
- What can you do to ensure that you reduce your workload when it comes to planning?

# 5  Expectations

Getting your expectations right is one of the most important things about teaching. If you truly want to simplify your life and reduce your workload, teaching your students good habits and getting your classroom environment right is key.

You'll hear that everywhere and quite often it isn't much help. We all know that a calm, stable environment is ideal for learning, but in the real world it's a bit more complicated than just a few minor tweaks. Depending on your subject, your context, the systems within your school and your own personal ethos and ideals, your expectations will differ from those of other teachers. Before we look at expectations, it might be a good idea to consider what we actually mean by the term, as it is thrown around in a number of guises in education.

An expectation, most simply defined by its root, is what you expect of any student in your class in any situation. Quite often, expectations are linked with behaviour (even though in the Teacher Standards there is a clear differentiation between these two). Because of this, it is easy to think that *expectation* refers predominantly to behaviour management and quickly teachers fall into the trap of focusing their efforts and attention on ensuring that behaviour meets expectations. Ironically, this often reduces productivity and progress of students as they aren't always clear with what the teacher (you) wants them to do in different situations.

As adults and specialists in our subjects it's easy to take for granted the expectations around a task or a skill, especially when we are aware of the outcome of goal. Quite often, students have a significantly smaller overview of the lesson, scheme of work or year and therefore they need more guidance on how to achieve the goal.

## Just behaviour?

Expectations should link to learning as well as behaviour. Furthermore, expectations should link to the skills that you are asking students to apply. By having laser-focused academic expectations, you heighten your level of control over the class and in turn their learning will become more focused. Although it is easiest to instil this with a new class (the September dream), it's also possible to retain students throughout the year, so don't panic! The main thing is that once you have set the expectations, you maintain consistency.

It isn't a matter of a magic list. The bespoke nature of teaching means that you need to be comfortable with what you want and before we go any further with the specifics of expectations, you need to reflect on what you want from your classes – you can't set and maintain expectations if you don't think carefully about them:

- What is the most important thing for you with regard to the outcome of a lesson?
- Which systems does your school have in place that you must follow with regard to expectations?
- How do you want students to feel in your classroom?
- Do you think your students understand what your expectations are for talking, writing, reading?
- Do you have any non-academic expectations?
- What are your expectations of yourself?
- Setting the standard – where are your lines?

Setting expectations can be a tricky business. I suppose back in the day, way back when, teachers may have got students to sign contracts and other such things, promising that they'd behave appropriately in class. I don't think this level of formalisation is a particularly effective or efficient use of your time. You certainly need to set your own standards for learning but there are a number of ways you can do this implicitly as well as explicitly.

First and most importantly, you need to decide what your expectations are. This may sound intuitive, but often different teachers will have different expectations and knowing yours means that you can draw your lines in the sand and, most importantly, stick to them. Too many times, I've seen NQTs and early career teachers struggling because they are trying to replicate the expectations of others and they simply can't sustain them because they conflict with the teacher's own personality so much.

## Less can be more

When considering your expectations, think sustainably. Too many expectations can get confusing for students and vague expectations can often be manipulated with the old, "Oh you didn't say…". You need to set your expectations and then essentially enforce them. I tend to try and avoid such militaristic language when talking about the classroom as I don't want to portray it as a battleground as such, but there will be some degree of power swaying when you try to establish yourself – it's totally normal for it not to work from day one… or more typically, work for two weeks then go south.

It is also a good idea to think about your expectations for behaviour and learning as two separate entities that are intrinsically linked. There are some expectations in my classroom that are givens and the students are fully aware of this. Being polite as they enter and leave is a staple. I start and end every lesson saying *hello* and *goodbye* – it sounds so simple but actually having expectations around our young people being good human beings prepares them for later life and it gives them a sense of stability that some of them crave so badly. Other expectations such as *please* and *thank you* aren't negotiable with me, neither is moving around the classroom or talking over each other. Are these explicit teaching expectations? No, they're just general expectations and correcting any behaviours that break the expectations is of paramount importance to me. I want learners to feel safe in my classroom and instead of telling them off if they don't "comply", I simply ask them why I don't like what they are doing. Compliance isn't conducive to a good learning environment. I'm in the nurturing business, not the soul crushing trade and I think modelling good manners and communication is a key part of our jobs. If you get the basics right the rest will follow. Strangely, these expectations are an incredible behaviour management tool. The students respond really respectfully, not because I've told them to but because I have taught them the importance.

## Clarity is key

With that said, you need to be clear when you set behavioural expectations. If your school doesn't have a clear policy that documents what crime constitutes which punishment, it might be a good idea to put something together for yourself. The reason being is that you can then be consistent and for any child this is key. Consistent behaviour management means that you are able to keep things fair and children actually respond really well to the idea of equality. When it comes to behavioural expectations, there should be no exceptions, ever. If consistency is key, then everyone must be treated exactly the same. Having clear parameters means that you are able to effectively manage the behaviour in your classroom and the clarity means that learning is kept at the forefront as opposed to haggling and sporadically scattered discipline. I'm conscious of floating into the realms of behaviour management and I don't want to do that but I do want to say that behavioural expectations need to be upheld to ensure that all students get the opportunity to learn in a safe environment.

Considering your academic expectations of pupils is another very important consideration. This may range from where you want them to write the date to how they underline work all the way to how they respond to an extended answer. Students are incredibly malleable but they are also often lacking common sense when it comes to learning. Being explicit with your academic expectations gives your tasks clarity and ensures that students are aware of what the outcome of their learning is. Again, you need to be consistent with this and you need to ensure your expectations are being met or they will quickly fall on deaf ears. The last thing you want to do is look at your books to see that students have just gone rogue on you without you noticing. Again, being tight around academic expectations is an incredible behavioural tool as any ambiguity about task expectations can quickly lead to disengagement. This may spark trouble. Avoid it completely by making your expectations crystal clear and buy in yourself.

## Engagement

I suppose that the biggest challenge for any teacher is truly engaging their students. Brophy and Good (1986) highlight the intrinsic link between academic engagement time and achievement, emphasising the importance of keeping students thinking. With all the plates spinning it can sometimes be soul destroying when the students just won't engage with what you are putting in front of them, especially when you know that their achievement will be affected. You see the planning time going down the drain and when you know time is tight, disengagement can be a real demotivator for teachers and detract from outcomes for students.

Time after time, I've observed incredibly talented teachers, who know their subjects inside out, fail to help pupils progress in lessons. Most of the time, it's down to one key factor: engagement.

So why do pupils become disengaged? Which barriers are causing this breakdown in learning? What can we do to ensure we keep our pupils engaged?

### Get the accessibility right

The first and most important (in my opinion) thing to consider when we are reflecting on engagement is the pitch of the tasks in a lesson. Too hard and you'll lose the class because they can't access the work; too easy and you'll lose them to distraction. Pitching a lesson perfectly means that you can avoid off-topic behaviour that stems from disengagement.

A sure-fire way to create accessible tasks is to layer in levels of challenge. Extensions, knowledge boosts and challenges are all ways you can build on the main task that is set.

By offering varying degrees of access, pupils are able to focus on their learning with less threat of becoming disengaged. I don't for a moment mean make five separate worksheets or anything ridiculous like that, instead think about layering tasks using different levels of questioning or focus on well-formulated sentences to summarise ideas.

Being able to read the class is a skill all teachers benefit from. Being too rigid in your planning and teaching leads to a lack of responsiveness – this can be hugely demotivating for pupils, especially if the proposed course isn't as effective as first anticipated. Having some flexibility as a teacher allows you to respond to the pupils' needs as they arise. If the class haven't processed a concept, it makes no sense to move onto the next step in their learning. Sometimes you need to wing it and you need students to feel safe enough to let you know they don't understand an idea. Taking the time to address misconceptions and having the confidence to divert from the plan if required means that you can maintain control over those who may have been lost if you'd moved on.

Seeing the finish line in a race gives you that burst to make the final push. Education isn't hugely different… it's just a much longer race. Having clear reasoning for why learning is taking place allows students to see the reason for their time and effort being invested. Having a good idea of the validity and context of learning allows a more focused drive. We all know that importance of outcomes over shorter periods of time, but it's also hugely important to consider the long game and how important is to make students aware of why they are learning. Having no goal can lead to complacency and this in turn can be a factor that leads to disengagement.

Keeping a class engaged is a juggling act. Actually telling if they are engaged is another battle altogether. Often, early career teachers assume that silence means engagement. I think the safe haven of silence gives an initial impression of control, but actually if we are looking at teaching more effectively and efficiently, we need to look at whether silence is an indicator of engagement or compliance.

## Compliance or engagement?

Children are exceptionally good at looking like they are thinking, for me there's nothing more frustrating than thinking that a class has understood something wholeheartedly form the vigorous nods, note-taking and smiles, for me to then test the knowledge to find they know little more than they did when we started. Checking for understanding is vital to ensure students are engaged with their learning. Pepper questioning, quick-fire written responses, low-stakes testing and, of course, longer responses are all ways to ascertain if students are actually engaged and, once again, it's absolutely vital that you are aware in your room and that you don't hide behind your desk. Getting in and amongst the class means that you are able to see if students are really engaging with the content in your lessons.

- How do you know your students are engaged?
- What do you look for to see that they are progressing?
- Can you explain how different approaches engage different classes?

Don't for a second think that you need to be all-singing, all-dancing to maintain engagement. Having some personality and passion for your subject helps, but don't focus on being a showperson, think more about how your expectations for engagement can be met through the tasks you are planning. Students will never meet your expectations if you're asking them to do something that doesn't marry with what you expect.

## Consistency

Humans are habitual animals and children thrive on consistency in schools, especially those students who lack it elsewhere in their lives. Whatever you decide with regard to your personal expectations, and no matter how you get them engaged, just make sure you stay consistent with it.

Don't let things slip when you get tired after a month or so, that's when your expectations come into play with regard to your workload.

If you have them established and you maintain them, in the long run you will save yourself loads of battles and hours of time that you would have to spend righting wrongs. Keeping everything consistent across the year is one of the key factors for success. In the past, I've had to change things throughout the year, as a leader and as a teacher. Deep down, I knew those changes would impact my students, no matter how minimal, and sometimes there's nothing you can do about altering the consistency. The most important thing is you do your best to maintain your expectations.

Consistency creates fairness and this in turn gives students a level playing field in the classroom. Even as adults we look for loopholes with things. Right now, I'm looking for a loophole for my speeding ticket that I just got… but there isn't one. I'm not saying that you need to base your classroom expectations around (crafty) traps that are put there to teach students lessons, what I'm saying is that if there is no wiggle room in the expectation, there is no room for debate to detract from the learning. Just like me doing 35 in a 30 zone, students who know the expectations can't really argue with them and when they do, they will hold their hands up… hopefully.

The dream, of course, is embedding the same consistency in teaching and learning expectations across the school so that regardless of subject or teacher, the students know the expectations. Strangely, this utopia isn't far off for us at the moment at my school, it's taken some hard graft and a lot of reflection on practice but it's happening, and it all started from a group of teachers consolidating their expectations and disseminating them. As early career teachers, you may not think that your expectations have an impact on others, but I can assure you that they do. Moreover, by being reflective and creating consistency in your classroom, you can model to others how they can reduce their workload with regard to this. Efficiency quickly spreads with regard to expectations and with some careful consideration, you can amplify your teaching by simply making the most of your learning time.

- How consistent are you?
- What could make you more consistent with your expectations?

## Praise

Naturally we want to give praise to children. Getting (and giving) praise is a real motivator and can build up confidence and character. Positivity facilitates motivation and when used correctly, praise is a powerful tool in the classroom, but the use of praise needs to be managed sensitively. Praise can hugely impact the dynamic in the classroom, and not always in the way that we hope (Dweck, 1999). You don't want to make more work for yourself by having something that is so seemingly positive backfire on you… and it can if you aren't careful.

When I was training and during my NQT year I got contradictory messages about praise. There were those who told me not to smile or be nice until Christmas and those who said to praise, praise, praise as much as you can. What I have come to realise over my teaching career is that controlled praise is a hugely effective way to improve behaviour, increase effort and engagement and, in turn, create more positive outcomes.

As a linguist, I concern myself with the intricacies of language (much to my wife's delight). Something you can really think about is how you give praise and why you give praise – strangely it can have a huge impact on the dynamic in your class. Thinking about praise has really changed the way I motivate students. I think previously I was lightly frivolous with my praise and the impact was that it was less effective than it could have been.

You'll hear loads of different phrases when it comes to praising students. Some are better than others for a number of reasons.

"This is one of the best responses in the class…"

"Excellent, outstanding…"

"You are so clever…"

"You can just do the Extension Task for this…"

- What is each of the above saying to a student (really)?
- Can any of the above help a student with their work?
- Do any of the above phrases motivate? How?

On the face of it, the comments are all positive, but when you think more about what is implied to the student being spoken to and those around them, the praise becomes less constructive and in fact in some cases becomes destructive to a good, safe working environment. Whimsical praise often loses its value and overuse of superlatives means that you quite literally end up wasting your breath. As Dweck (2012) found, overpraising can actually have self-defeating consequences.

## Linguistic economy

The idea of linguistic economy is something that most teachers don't pay much heed to. When we think about workload, we focus so much on the written workload and the time put in with physical resources and books, that we neglect to remember that talk and voice (besides knowledge) are a teacher's main tools. Over-using your words reduces the impact of them. Teacher talk has been a hotly debated topic over the past few years – not enough, too much, it's always back and forth. That debate aside, consider when you are teaching why you are saying something. A startling amount of the time, you won't be able to justify why you have said what you have. Think about your vocal workload as well as your written workload. Praise is a good place to start, is your praise having an impact on the learning or the motivation of the students? No? Then stop doing it and do something else. Think about linguistic economy – does it need to be said?

I'm in no way saying don't praise (or talk). On the contrary, I'm simply saying, think about how you praise and talk, like I say, it can have a huge impact on the experience of students in your lessons.

Making your praise effective and efficient doesn't take away from the personability, it adds to the impact and that's what we are in the classroom for. There are a few things that you can do to help you make your praise more impactful.

## Be specific with praise

You need to be very specific; just like written feedback, praise can act as an indicator of success, but only if it refers to the point that is worthy of the praise. Make sure you identify exactly what is "excellent" about a response. By using a more specific phrase and linking the positivity to an exact point in the work, the student knows precisely what they are being praised for. This reinforces positive practice and ensures that praise isn't misinterpreted (consolidating misconceptions) and also avoids the praise sounding whimsical. Celebrating good work or exceptional effort is motivational, but for it to have the long-lasting impact you want, make your comments as efficient as possible.

Focusing praise on effort and process can be a lot more effective than praising ability. Creating a sense of growth and positivity around effort and resilience is something that can really help build student character and perseverance towards tasks. Reconsidering how I praise for effort drastically reduced the ever-present defeatism in some of my less confident students. Building an expectation around determination is something that links directly with the idea of desirable difficulty. If we are to use the theory in our teaching, we must ensure that learners don't give up or opt out when the difficulty makes them think more deeply. Praise can ensure that students remain motivated and focused on the target through reassurance and support. Moving away from praising ability means that we also move away from failure being something that is excused by something that is innate – you'll not believe how much time, effort and emotion this tiny shift in your praise will have on your workload.

Making sure that behavioural praise focuses on what's going right instead of what's going wrong is of paramount importance. For me, behaving generally isn't something that needs to be praised as it should be an expectation in your classroom. What I think needs praising is behaviour towards learning. As teachers, I think we sometimes shy away from words based around skills in fear of students not "getting them", but building a sense of commonality around your language use in praise, feedback and in class discussions creates a stable learning environment for those in your classroom. Entertaining any kind of bad behaviour and taking time to address it detracts from the learning, so don't be afraid to highlight that to the students, but do it positively. Creating a safe working environment is your job and you are the boss of that space. It's your domain and you need to use to praise to ensure that you are able to avoid behavioural issues.

## Parents

An underutilised resource of schools is parents. A number of studies have suggested the strong correlation between parental involvement (and interest in their child's learning) and successful outcomes (Son & Strasser, 2002; Sylva et al., 2004, 2008). Including parents in the learning process and empowering them to help their children is a brilliant way to reduce the workload of teachers. There are a number of factors that you need to bear in mind if you are to take advantage of this additional resource, however.

First and foremost, you have to remember that some parents will have hated school. In some cases, if you work in a school that has been through a period of rapid improvement, there may also be a huge level of prejudice towards the school, especially if they cannot shift the label of old. Finally, just like the children you teach, parents have varying abilities and commitments to their children. Regardless of the above, having a plan for involving parents in your teaching is smart.

Most parents want their children to succeed in education – this isn't the issue. The issue in reality is the lack of parental understanding regarding the ins and outs of what is expected of students and, more importantly, how they get them to do what is expected of them at home. Parenting is a full-time job, often on top of a full-time job. Parents often don't have the luxury of time to read books on teaching and learning.

One of the most common requests from parents/carers to you as a teacher will inevitably be: "How can I help my child at home?" This question has a habit of popping up at parents' evenings, open events and (shockingly) directly after presentations about "helping your children at home". Considering it and having a plan will allow you to implement additional learning and, if set up right, there'll be no extra work in it for you.

Reports. A necessary evil for most – the word alone makes me shudder. But how high is the impact of written report? I'd say pretty minimal, but we aren't here to slate approaches, we are here to consider how we can reduce workload and sometimes that means working within remits that are out or our control.

If you have to write reports then you need parents to get the most out for them for them to be worthy of your time. When you write your reports, make sure you use accessible language. Don't throw reams of jargon and sophistication into the report in a draconian attempt to sound authoritative and powerful. Furthermore, remember that what may seem a commonly understood phrase or term to you as a professional could still be complete jargon to a non-professional. Remembering that parents may have hated school or have had bad experiences, you don't want them turning straight off – that's a total waste of your time. Instead stick to the basics: what is going well, what needs improving specifically, how to improve specifically. Written reports have their advantages. They can act as a resource that parents can look back over, it gives the parent a starting point for helping at home and it is specific to your subject.

## Teaching parents to be (better) teachers

Your job is to teach and to mould young people into good members of society. To add to our woes, parents often try to enforce their own experiences of school when "helping" their children at home. Conjuring images of the cane and inkpot-laden wooden desks won't take you to a good mental place – no, no, no. First off and quite simply, you should encourage parents/carers to be positive. Creating a supportive and positive atmosphere about education at home can make a real difference in how homework and school tasks are undertaken. This can range from simple praise when some work is done, to more subtle approaches such as asking "when would you like to revise?" rather than demanding "why aren't you revising?". Or "talk me through what you have done so far" rather than "you haven't done much". Educating parents on how they can help at home can really help you in the classroom. One of my favourite little tricks are knowledge organisers with explicit learning instructions at the top. Coupled with a text home listing expectations, this learning resource has had a massive impact on knowledge retention in my classes. It's cost me a bit of time designing the knowledge organiserand getting it printed, but the impact has been so impressive.

On the theme of communication, another way in which you can engage parents is to keep them informed. Aligning your expectations with what parents should expect at home establishes more consistency for learners. There is nothing to say that you can't make your expectations explicit for what you want students to be doing at home (if you can fit it in with your school policy) and make parents aware of these expectations. Parents' evenings traditionally focus so much on what the students are doing in class, why not spin that and use the time to help parents understand what they can do to help their children at home? My advice is that any communication you have with parents needs to be minimalist in terms of how much time it takes them. By this I mean you can't assume that they have any prerequisites to educating their child effectively. Giving a parent some simple exercises for recall testing from a knowledge organiser or an approach for getting their child to explain something to them with some phrases to get them started are really valuable, or even if it's encouraging them to spend five minutes in the evening discussing what their child has learned that day. It all has an impact and any work they do outside of school reduces your burden.

- Have you communicated with parents about what they can do to help at home?
- What would you ask them to do if you did?
- What kind of materials would suit your parents in your context?

## Expectations of teachers

One thing we often forget as teachers is that along with the expectations we set in the classroom, we also often set expectations for ourselves without realising it. By our very nature, teachers also have a set of expectations placed upon them by leadership, by parents and, of course, by external agencies.

One thing we need to do if we are truly going to teach smart is control and rein in the expectations we place upon ourselves and, if appropriate, question those placed upon us by others. I'm not saying that there needs to be a riot, but teaching is a high enough pressure job with 30 children in a classroom, let alone when you add in the additional factors.

Be realistic with yourself. There is a very fine line between dedication and stupidity. Prioritising tasks is a skill that you must learn and then master if you are to reduce your workload. Consider the following tasks, which would you say are necessary and which are unnecessary?

- Marking books
- Correcting grammar and spellings
- Planning a SoW
- Printing resources
- Eating
- Preparing for an AP
- Making a cup of tea
- Sorting your classroom displays
- Buying new highlighters

Hold on, you may think, all of those are necessary tasks… that's the point. Any job you have will have a reason, even if it is something as trivial as restocking highlighters, what you need to think about is how much impact this is going to have on your teaching, how much impact will it have on the students and how much time do you have to complete the task? Making a priority hierarchy, also known commonly as a list, can put things into perspective. You can't expect yourself to be able to do everything at once. Sometimes at school, you don't get a minute, and that's fine, but when you do, make sure you prioritise the tasks that are most important… and yes, in most cases it should be eating or having a cup of tea.

### Don't lose touch with reality

Having high expectations for yourself is one thing, but that doesn't have to mean always working. Knowing when enough is enough is the key to ensuring that you stay in the profession. Overworking yourself often leads to you being counterproductive. Part of the reason I wanted to write this book was actually because I often work with and for people who can't see that they are adding no value to their teaching or their students' learning by working inefficiently.

Having high expectations with regard to your teaching should be focused on the effectiveness of your presence in the classroom and sometimes that means getting a good night's kip. Teaching is a profession that is vulnerable to the snowball effect. Work seems to creep into evenings, evenings then turn into nights and before long, work never stops. Take time to reflect on if it's actually worth the additional time you are putting in. Being fractionally more austere with yourself can, in the long run, be significantly more beneficial to you, your family and the children you teach.

- How do you know when you are tired?
- When do you stop working?
- What are you own expectations of yourself?
- How many of the expectations have you put upon yourself and how many are organisational?

# 6 Feedback

Feedback is one of a teacher's main tools that they can call upon to help their students further progress in their learning. Bellon et al. (1991) state that, "Feedback is more strongly and consistently related to achievement than any other teaching behaviour […] this relationship is consistent regardless of grade, socioeconomic status, race, or school setting." But feedback normally comes at a cost – namely an increase in workload.

As specialists, the ability to identify errors and address misconceptions is a paramount part of moving learning forward and, quite often, allowing understanding and knowledge to be reflected on and consolidated. One of the most time-consuming jobs as a classroom practitioner is to mark and assess work and provide effective feedback on that work. Research suggests that one in six (17%) teachers in the UK are spending more than 11 hours a week on marking and assessments. Statistically, this amount of time spent reflecting on student work is significantly higher than most other countries (OECD, 2015).

Why though? Mostly because teachers aren't considering their practice as carefully as they could, but also it is because schools still have marking policies that are redundant and outdated.

Quite often, teachers spend hours marking books and giving feedback that is never responded to. Moreover, when feedback is responded to, the student has already moved on with their learning, instantly rendering the content provided by the teacher useless. An alternative to the approach of giving feedback to students outside of lessons is to provide it in the lesson, as they work. This is not a new concept. Verbal feedback has been a part of classroom practice for centuries, but the verbal aspect of feedback quite often is forgotten and cannot be reflected on due to the nature of the medium in which it is delivered. Getting feedback right is so important as using the wrong approaches can actually be detrimental to the process of learning (Butler, 1987; Kluger & DeNisi, 1998; McColskey & Leary, 1985).

Ask yourself these questions:

- How long do you spend marking books outside of lessons?

- Why are you marking books?

- What are you looking for?

- Is your feedback measurable?

- Can you see the impact of your feedback?

No matter how you mark, you need to ask yourself two big questions:

- Is the marking or feedback benefiting the student's progress?

- Is it measurable?

Think to yourself: is my comment relevant? Does it extend learning? Can they understand how to improve their work? If you can say *yes* to all of these elements then your feedback will certainly be helping students move forward.

Second, think to yourself, how are they going to show me that they have understood and taken on-board my feedback? The hours spent on wasted comments and vague targets makes me hang my head in pity as I read through some exercise books. You can see your colleagues' proverbial blood, sweat and tears, but you know that nothing has been done with the hugely valuable time that has been spent marking. John Hattie (2012) highlights feedback as one of the more impactful factors on students' outcomes, but how do we make feedback less time-consuming and more effective?

## Making the distinction between marking and feedback

Quite understandably, there are situations in which we take words to be synonymous, but they are in fact not. The English language is made up of a huge amount of words that are interchangeable and this can sometimes lull us into assumptions, especially when it comes to concepts that seem aligned. In the classroom, errors and misconceptions are quite often mixed when in practice they are completely different ideas. Similarly, feedback and marking are often whimsically interchanged with one another. It may seem like a minor point of detail, but the concepts are hugely different and if teachers are serious about ensuring progress, each idea needs to be differentiated accordingly. Once you've divided the two, you can start thinking about what exactly it is that is creating workload and which approaches are having an impact where others are not.

### Misconceptions

In short, in terms of learning, a misconception is something that is incorrect because it is based on or at least derives from faulty thinking or understanding. Misconceptions often arise due to misunderstandings of concepts or ideas during teaching, missing conceptualisation (an idea is too abstract for a learner) and on some occasions from the delivery of the teacher.

Misconceptions are an inevitable part of teaching. By its very nature, teaching involves transmitting information from one person to another – we'd be superhuman if there were never any misunderstandings during this process. As teachers, there are a few approaches we can adopt to avoid *unnecessary* misconceptions:

- New information in small steps – breaking learning into small chunks allows learners to process the information they are being given more efficiently. It also allows the teacher to consolidate and build strong foundations before moving on.

- Provide models and scaffold tasks – ensuring that the tasks set are clear and students are support means that there is less chance of them becoming confused by the content and instructions. Moreover, scaffolding and models reduce the extraneous load, meaning students are less likely to become cognitively overloaded.
- Review learning regularly – by revisiting concepts and ideas, students' knowledge becomes more compounded and it is less likely misconceptions will occur over time from simply forgetting details.

Feedback is the best way to help students address misconceptions. The type of feedback you use is defined by your subject and style of teaching, the important thing, however, is that you are able to identify and, in some cases, track the misconceptions a class or an individual have. Repeated misconceptions lead to errors.

### Errors

Although errors can (and most often do) stem from misconceptions, they are a very different concept all together. An error is a mistake – it is the process by which you get something wrong. In learning, errors often arise from the application of the learning that has taken place. Errors can be a result of misconceptions, but the two ideas differ hugely and errors are identified and dealt with in a different way.

Errors are highlighted through marking. It's very difficult to identify an error without having a definitive (albeit often subjective) answer first. In the classroom, errors highlight progress and often equate to quantitative data. Similarly to misconceptions, errors must be addressed in order for learning to take place and quite often there is more of a negative stigma attached to them, but they are by no means less or more important than misconceptions.

The glaringly obvious issue is that we deal with misconceptions and errors in very different ways. Marking and feedback are very separate approaches and if we use the wrong one at the wrong time, learners make less progress in terms of their knowledge and understanding.

Avoiding misconceptions, or at least trying to reduce them means that there will be fewer errors made. The two ideas are intrinsically linked, but they are certainly not the same.

- Can you identify between an error and misconception in a student's work or in their verbal response?

- Do you embed enough opportunities to pick up on both misconceptions and errors, or do you focus on one more than the other?

## Monitoring tasks

Something that has really impacted my practice in recent years is reflecting on the way in which tasks are monitored in my classroom. Striking a balance between encouraging independent practice and guiding learning is sometimes tricky, especially with the time constraints imposed upon us as teachers. There are, of course, numerous ways in which you can monitor and intervene with the learning taking place, but here are a few of the considerations that have made my monitoring of tasks more productive.

Teaching new topics will inevitably lead to misconceptions. Pre-planning for these misconceptions is a good way to ensure that students are not overwhelmed and that you are able to intervene when required. It can be argued that if you know what the misconceptions are going to be, you should plan to avoid them... of course, but regardless of the planning, misconceptions will arise. Vocabulary, concepts and ideas that have proved to be difficult in the past, or you as a professional know are sticking points in the topic can then be looked out for during the lesson. Monitoring of the understanding and progress in these areas then means that bigger misconceptions are less likely to arise from our teaching and fewer students are likely to become disengaged.

The reality is that preconceived misconceptions may or may not arise. Our awareness of them potentially occurring doesn't mean they will always be problem. Teaching is a responsive business and often misconceptions arise where (and when) we don't expect them. Monitoring for actual misconceptions and addressing them as learning is taking place means that learning becomes more efficient. By circulating the classroom as students are working, teachers are able to highlight any individual issues, but also they can pick up on wider issues that may have arisen for the whole class. Coming away from your plan is really important – there is no point moving on and not addressing the issues. These issues are bound to be consolidated and more difficult to address at a later time. Moreover, we can't expect students to complete complex tasks if we haven't ensured they have a firm base of understanding. Monitoring for misconceptions in the lesson hugely reduces your workload after the lesson too.

On the topic of workload, if you're giving feedback in the lesson, you're marking. Taking the opportunity to read your students' work while you're circulating and monitoring tasks means that you can provide them with the feedback they need to overcome issues, or allow them to stretch themselves further. You may not get round the whole class in one lesson, but over a week, it's possible to give feedback to students while they are learning, with the added bonus of them instantly being able to respond to your feedback. Effective monitoring means you can intervene at the point an individual most requires it. Feedback also becomes about improving student skills and less about improving an individual piece of work. The merits of this approach for students and teachers are not celebrated enough.

Can you evidence how well you monitor tasks? Is it possible to measure? Does it really matter? In the past, we've always been pressured in to evidencing the impact we are having on learning. With the assumed inevitability (and mythical?) expectation that Ofsted will be looking with a microscope at the way in which we have monitored our students in class.

Effective circulation is evidenced in student confidence and the atmosphere in your classroom, not through written evidence in books. By effectively monitoring your students' learning, you are also modelling how they should monitor themselves. One of the biggest shifts in self-awareness I have noticed in my classroom has come about from the way in which I constantly circulate and intervene with my students when need arises. Making your input explicit trains them to become more rigorous with their own checking of their work against outcomes. Stepping away from the book-based evidence has been really empowering and it has actually significantly changed the types of discussions I have with students when monitoring.

How each teacher chooses to monitor their class is down to personal preference, but are you making the most of this valuable time?

- What do you do while your students work?
- Do you record how you monitor tasks?
- Do you need to record how you monitor tasks and the input you have had?

## Live feedback

Every year, there is a fad that claims to reduce marking workload: verbal feedback stampers, marking codes and many, many more approaches are incorporated in an attempt to more easily facilitate the onslaught of book-based input from teachers.

Typically, it isn't long before teachers realise that a lot of these approaches aren't useful for student progress, instead they are simply box-ticking exercises. Ofsted wants to see evidence of marking – give it a tick. This is no good. Marking and feedback is so much more than a box-ticking exercise.

The truth is, quality reigns over quantity. Observers aren't (or at least shouldn't be) looking to see if every page has some teacher input on it, instead they should be looking for how the feedback and marking is helping students to improve.

Up until this point, I have always focused on feedback methods, disregarding anything else. I'm convinced that using questions as feedback in the short term (so the pupils have something to respond to) and focused targets in the long term are the best ways to help pupils progress.

Experience has shown that this approach is effective over time. But, and this is the thing that has me excited, I would never consider exactly "when" I was feeding back and marking.

Feedback needs to be instant. It needs to be given and acted upon straight away or it's not having the optimum impact. Think about it.

You mark your books every two weeks, you give excellent feedback tasks to extend learning, but is your feedback as effective as it could be? Is that pupil in the same mindset they were when they were completing that piece of work? Is their response going to be a bolt-on that ticks a box?

It is more than likely that although it looks smart, your feedback isn't helping as much as it could. In addition, how much time outside lessons has it taken you to plough through those books? Too long. But how on earth can you give effective feedback and save time?

The key is simply to mark and feedback in-class while students are working. It seems obvious, but it takes practice and planning.

For every book you can see in the lesson, you save yourself a significant amount of time outside the lesson, reducing the burden of marking and in turn reducing the pressure of the teaching workload.

You might not get through the whole class in a lesson, but over the week you can see every student's book.

Traditionally, teachers would mark books outside of the classroom after lessons. This is ineffective for a number of reasons. The most notable, any time you spend working outside the classroom decreases your time for other things, but beside this there are other factors such as the redundancy of feedback once a task has been completed. Why would you write the same three comments after having read 30 books from one of your classes?

No exaggeration, my books are marked more and with higher quality feedback than they have ever been before – and I've not spent one minute in the last term marking outside of lessons. That sounds like a horrific sound bite that my current employer will hate, but actually, it shows just how effective you can be in the classroom if you're on the ball and making the most of your lesson time.

But how do you do it? It's simple (well it's still a difficult adjustment but the theory is simple), when the pupils are working on a directed task, you simply circulate and give them personal questions/tasks in their books to complete. Extension tasks, synthesis questions and questions to put right misconceptions are used depending on the task. It's differentiated, individual feedback that can be responded to instantly – and that's what makes it so effective. The students respond to it straightaway. It's current, it's relevant, they can see their progress and so can the teacher. The process works like this:

- Read a student's work.

- Ask them a question or a series of questions about what they have written. These questions can be literacy-based, testing technical knowledge, synthesis questions, hypothetical questions or simply one-word questions such as "why?" Alternatively, you may model the start of the next paragraph for them in their books.

- The pupils respond to your question or the stimulus you have given them.

There are, and will continue to be, people who doubt that it is possible to mark books like this. Let me just add some extra contextual detail about how this method has been developed. I work in what some may call a challenging school and this approach has had a positive impact on behaviour and attitude to learning. The constant attention to detail and work has boosted the level of engagement significantly in extended writing tasks because, quite simply, students have no option but to succeed. If they encounter any issues, they know that I will be picking up on them, so they actually quite often self-moderate and are more open to asking for help.

It might be noted that I teach English and that this approach lends itself to extended writing; however, I've extensively applied this approach in science, maths and humanities – it works in those subjects too. Quite honestly, this approach has been a game-changer with regard to me reducing my workload.

I'm not naive enough to think that the majority of teachers can just decide to start a new way of marking whenever they want. More often than not, schools have feedback policies that ask for very specific criteria to be met. If this is constraining your practice, simply take live marking and make it fit what is expected of you. If your school is stuck in the dark ages of WWW and EBIs, then get reading the work in class and give out those dreaded EBIs before the work is finished so that the students at least has a chance to respond to your feedback while the task is still relevant to them. You may not have the freedom to change the policy, but you certainly should have the freedom to play the system in a way that benefits the students – get the feedback in as quickly as you can.

How you feedback and mark is, to an extent, a personal preference. Teachers have their own approaches. When you are marking, ask yourself how effective your practice is and how much of an impact it is having on pupil attainment and progress. Are your hours of marking outside lessons actually having an impact? Try to switch your approach to responding to need in the lesson, you'll soon see a huge shift in your workload.

- How much time do you spend out of lessons marking?
- How much of this marking has a direct impact on the task that the student was completing?
- Do you plan for feedback opportunities in lessons?
- Have you got a good understanding the success criteria for each topic that you teach?

## Whole-class feedback

The concept of feeding back to a whole class on a piece of work isn't something new. It has been around for years. But recently, it seems that there has been a realisation that if done properly, this can be a real time-saver in terms of teacher workload. I have experimented with this approach a lot and it has the potential to reduce marking significantly and when coupled with live marking, can be a perfect way to balance group and individualised feedback.

Identifying misconceptions is such a huge part of teaching. Traditionally, to achieve this, there has been an onus on teachers reading through piles of books with their coloured pens, ticking and crossing, setting targets, giving and giving individualised feedback. The issue is that quite often, teachers end up writing the same things over and over again. The likely causes (besides misunderstanding the task) are misconceptions that have arisen from the teaching or learning, and in most cases these are consistent across classes (to a degree of course.)

This is time-consuming and, in all honesty, not remotely effective practice if we consider progress and impact on pupils, not to mention the time spent looking at the same thing over and over again. If you're quick, you might blast through 30 books in an hour… but you're not really getting much bang for your buck.

Whole-class feedback, however, flips the tradition upside-down. It is about identifying common errors in work and addressing them collectively. If you are able to identify the misconception as students are working, why not address it there and then in the lesson? Give your feedback to the whole class as they are learning… not one minute spent out of class looking through books, not a globule of ink wasted on irrelevant comments that are quickly glanced over, just a misconception, addressed. What more could you ask for? What more could your class ask for?

Alternatively, if there is a common misconception occurring and you pick it up towards the end of the task, provide that feedback to the class at the start of the next lesson in the form of a hand-out or on a slide. You can then address the misconception and ensure it is overcome before you move on with learning and run the risk of it becoming embedded.

I will at this point issue a warning, however. To overcome a misconception, you as the teacher must teach the students what they need to do to avoid it. You then must give them the opportunity to apply the skill or idea in a different context to see if they have indeed overcome it. If not, have the confidence to start the cycle again. Just think of all of the time you have saved from flicking through books!

Critics argue that this approach destroys individualised feedback and can hinder the progress of the highest achievers, due to them not having a misconception in the first place. Those concerns are valid, but only if whole-class feedback is used badly. I argue that repeating skills that you can already do and highlighting the misconceptions of others allows learners to recap skills and consolidate their successes – so what if five students didn't have the misconception, the exercise is still valid, they get to reapply the skill and test if they really understood it first time round.

When done well, whole-class feedback can save hours of teacher time and significantly improve student outcomes. But it is in danger of being seen as a fad because it is misunderstood. I have seen so many different approaches on Twitter that act as a tick box. Don't use this approach as a tick box, I repeat *do not use it as a tick box*. If you don't use whole-class feedback effectively, it becomes a lead weight and students will quickly disengage because they won't see the merit in it, so handle with care.

Many have misconceptions around how whole-class feedback works. The term itself is a bit ambiguous because it implies everyone gets the same feedback. That may be the case for elements of the feedback, but it is often tailored to groups or individuals within the class, if it isn't then it should be. Whole-class feedback can take a number of forms, and it doesn't just have to deal with one misconception that has arisen, and as with anything in education, the idea is just the start – it's about how the concept is applied that makes all the difference. Whole-class feedback is only effective if a teacher, department or school think carefully about what they need in their context.

Often, teachers opt for sheets, slides or exercises to provide the feedback in a way in which focuses on one or a number of the following elements:

- Misconception
- Extensions
- New material
- Praise
- Advice
- Models
- Alternative interpretations
- Key vocabulary

No matter what the approach is, if it helps students progress and is costing less teacher time, it is serving a more practical function than most traditional "long" marking.

There is nothing saying that whole-class feedback can't be coupled with another approach. For example, I do weekly whole-class feedback coupled with live marking each lesson and in total it costs me approximately zero hours outside the classroom. The trick is to be organised and to make the most of your class time. Don't be static behind your desk (assuming you still have it after Chapter 3) get in amongst it and do your marking when it is most needed – while kids are working.

Too many teachers see marking as a strain and a burden. Whole-class feedback can be the remedy to that problem, but only if we protect it from becoming a fad by reiterating how to do it well, and not letting a watered-down version undermine it.

## Peer feedback

Another way to reduce your feedback workload is to train students efficiently to do the job for you. Salles (2016) succinctly summarises the ways in which a teacher can reduce their workload by effectively using your knowledge and specialism to help students highlight issues in each other's work.

In honesty, peer feedback is a tool I have been under-utilising in my classroom. As with most teachers, my practice goes through waves of change and often you forget about certain approaches, or at least forget about the merits of certain approaches. For me, peer feedback is one of those.

I'm a big believer in quick (instant where possible) feedback and well set up peer assessment tasks are a sure-fire way to ensure that students get timely feedback on tasks. The thing is, students helping students is a minefield if not handled properly – that's why you need to consider your feedback tasks carefully and think about why you might use them.

Feedback has got to be timely and any delay significantly reduces its effectiveness. If you leave feedback too long then it loses its value and importance, simply because students forget what they were doing or why they did it. Leaving work unchecked can also send the message that it lacks importance. One of the huge pros to peer feedback is that it can be integrated into lessons and weaved between tasks to help students continually improve. These interventions can also be really snappy – much quicker than the teacher circulating the class looking for misconceptions.

If you have something to say then say it – that's the message with peer feedback. The feedback has to be specific and to the point with no beating around the bush, simply because students are susceptible to distraction. Training your classes to look for certain patterns in responses, heightening their awareness of vocabulary and directing them to look for specific features not only exemplifies how to approach the questions in the task, but it also gives them insight into how they themselves will be assessed. Correct training with regard to peer feedback is an exceptional way to top up and consolidate individual knowledge and skills.

Hattie and Timperley (2007) stress that that effective feedback answers three questions: Where am I going? How am I going [to get there]? Where to next? If students don't see their learning journey clearly, they won't buy into feedback tasks. It's really important that the students value the feedback they give and receive – they are, after all, the ones who will benefit most. By getting them to consider their own learning, you are also encouraging self-awareness, which is an exceptional skill to master, especially if we are aiming to encourage more independence.

If we don't give students the time to reflect on their feedback then they can't respond effectively and constructively and implement the given suggestions. Planning in time for modelling how to give feedback and also putting time aside for responding to the feedback means that the process becomes more valued. A rushed attempt at the end of a lesson in the form of a (massively outdated) plenary style exercise will inevitably have little impact.

Getting students away from the sense that their ability is fixed is hugely empowering. Effective peer feedback breeds a culture of growth and reinforces the idea that learning is a process that is about building on your strengths and overcoming your weaknesses. When students begin to appreciate the importance of the feedback from their peers, they allow themselves to grow as learners.

Failure is part of learning and abolishing the fear of failure is an important part of the learning process. I am a great believer in ensuring that you, as a teacher, package the feedback of failure in a way in that doesn't damage student wellbeing. Simply crossing a response or saying "no" to an answer isn't effective practice (regardless of how many times in their lives students will have to deal with these situations) and coming from a teacher, can do students some harm. Peer assessment is a great buffer for failure and it helps students identify and pick up on mistakes and misconceptions before their work gets to the teacher. Building up layers of success can work as a confidence builder for learners, especially as quite often, classmates are viewed as more collaborative than judgemental.

- Do you plan opportunities for peer feedback in your lessons?
- Have you got clear expectations for peer feedback?
- Do you trust students to identify errors and misconceptions in work?

# 7 Questioning

Questioning is an absolute art. There are no two ways around it, questioning is also one of the most difficult skills for new teachers (and experienced teachers) to truly master. To effectively question, you need a number of prerequisites. Some of these you can plan for and intentionally use in your practice, others require more attention over time.

Regardless of the subject you teach, using questioning effectively allows you to ascertain students' knowledge and understanding, check that understanding at different points in the lesson, stretch learning and most importantly of all, engage learners and keep them thinking. Memory is the residue of thought (Willingham, 2008), so if you want students to remember an idea, you really need them to think deeply about it and questioning is the key to doing this.

Asking a question isn't the be all and end all of this skill, and early in your teaching it's hard to see how you can have the capacity to spin this plate (along with all of the others) and help learners. If we break questioning down, there are some distinct elements that we know are required for the process to be successful – especially from the teacher's side.

- Subject knowledge
- Distribution patterns
- Having a commonality of language
- Using the right type of question
- Calling for response
- Set expectations around questioning

Ensuring that you consider these factors, you can reduce your workload by making your questioning more efficient. Workload isn't a beast that is instantly tameable and there can be (and will be) times where making your life a bit harder for a period of time will actually help you hugely in the long run. Your practice around questioning is one of those times. Small tweaks can be made and have an impact in the short term, but for you to get the most out of your questioning, you may have to step outside your comfort zone a bit. With that said, making your questioning more efficient and effective means that you have a better understanding of how your pupils are learning, and in turn, you are able to plan, give feedback and generally teach them in a more focused manner. Without making this seem a bit clichéd, if you crack questioning, you'll make massive strides with regard to reducing your workload overall.

We need to start somewhere, however. As classroom teachers, you'll be asking questions a lot already… but how effective are they? Ask yourself the following:

- Do you know the answers to all of the questions you ask?
- Why do you use questioning in your lessons?
- How often do you question each student in each lesson?
- Do you have any phrases that you use for questioning? Are these effective?
- What types of questioning approaches do you use?
- Do you have any explicit expectations around questioning?

Reflecting on your questioning can be a difficult task as quite often you don't explicitly plan for the questions you will ask. In fact to do so could massively impact your planning time and we aren't about adding to workload. To make your questioning more effective, you need to drill down and look at exactly what you do, because too often, questioning becomes habitual and an unintentional side effect of this is that questioning becomes a tick box exercise that doesn't scratch the surface of what could be achieved. This can make the learning in your classroom stagnate and we don't want any of the issues that we know arise when students lose engagement.

## Subject knowledge

I've seen some incredible teaching from non-specialists in different subjects. Subject knowledge is not the only thing that makes you a good teacher. I know people (as I'm sure you do) who are nothing short of geniuses... put them in front of a class of teenagers though and there is no way in the world they would be able to teach them a thing or engage them for more than a few seconds. *Subject specialist* is a term I tend to avoid as there is no real measure of what makes you "specialist" in a subject. It's pretty obvious that for some types of teaching there is a minimum requirement of knowledge that you need to be a teacher of that subject, but there are no hard and fast rules.

Teaching is about so much more than knowing your subject inside out, but to question effectively, you need to know your stuff – Ball (1991, p5) simply states "teachers cannot help children learn things they themselves do not understand". Specialist or not, you need to have a deep understanding of what you are teaching or you won't be able to question effectively. You may be able to plan a perfect series of questions, using exceptional phrasing and distribution, but if you can't understand the answers, you are negating the whole process. I think back to when I started teaching and the thought of getting answers to questions that I didn't understand really worried me. My degree is in linguistics and the concept of literature was something that remained abstract to me. I'd ask questions that were relatively narrow in order to get the answers I wanted and it quickly became evident to me when I was training that I needed to build up my confidence with the different texts I was teaching. Nobody wants to look silly in front of their class when they don't know the answer and no child wants their answer to trigger a bewildered look – not knowing your subject content well enough can be detrimental to both parties.

With the right amount of subject knowledge, questioning becomes endless in possibility. You need enough understanding and knowledge to be able to formulate the question and respond to any answer that you are given. Moreover, you need to have the confidence to be able to highlight what is right and wrong about the answer. Some of the most astounding misconceptions that students have come from ineffective or vague teacher questioning and response. Don't make your own life harder by not knowing your stuff – in the long run, addressing those misconceptions that have become embedded will take a lot longer than it would have for you to have read up on the topic that little bit more.

## Distribution

On the surface, questioning is something that is seen to target an individual student to test their knowledge. I suppose that'd be the definition that somebody who doesn't teach anymore might give. Questioning is about more than the individual though. If the questions are distributed and spaced effectively, a teacher can ascertain the understanding of a whole class in a very small window of time.

There are no hard and fast rules when it comes to how many questions teachers should use in each phase of questions, or when those phases should occur, but something that is of importance is how many of the class are involved in being questioned. Each student in the class needs to come up with an answer to the question before the response is asked for or the thinking ratio of the class will be too low. Children are clever when it comes to this, and your approach to questioning can be quickly figured out if you're not careful. Simply asking every student in the class a singular question each lesson isn't enough because they know that once they've had their turn, they can switch off. Avoiding phrases such as, "Who haven't I asked today?" ensures that students stay engaged remain thinking… because that's the real point of questioning, it stimulates thinking.

That's the thing you need to remember, the vocalisation of a singular response is only one output. Questioning needs to make the students think and ensuring you distribute your questions accordingly will heighten the thinking ratio.

Moreover, a well thought-through distribution of questions will also increase participation. The fairer the questioning feels to the students, the more likely they are to feel safe in your classroom. Repeatedly asking the same student the hard questions to validate your own teaching is counterproductive and gives you an unrepresentative sampling of the understanding of the class.

So how can you vary the distribution of questions in your lessons? First, you need to know your students and second, you need to be able to be versatile and adapt. Taking into account Bjork's ideas around desirable difficulty, you need to be able to adapt questions to suit individual learners and not make the questions too easy or too hard for them. Distribute your questions evenly and make sure that you ask questions that stimulate thinking across the class. Using action words such as *why*, *how*, *counter*, you can increase the pace and move the questioning round in a fluid manner. The first question asked needs to be the basis for the discussion, but then you need to facilitate the discussion and the exploration. You need to steer the responses in a way that gets the best out of the students. My advice is don't shy away from individuals, this just strengthens stigmas. Creating a culture of answering is of paramount importance. If you can get a colleague to watch you teach and map your question distribution over a phase in your lesson, you can test how good you are at this. If they get lost because you've asked so many questions, you've won.

Don't think of question distribution just in terms of patterns and who you are asking questions, but think about how you distribute your questioning time. To distribute questions effectively, you must master wait time. Consider this:

Teacher: Josh, what's the capital of England?

versus

Teacher: What's the capital of England? [Wait five seconds] Josh?

What does the wait time allow? It lets the students all think about the question and the answer they will give – all of them – and then one of them is picked. Instead of every child except Josh switching off, the whole class has had to consider their answer. The participation ratio is increased 30-fold and you have made the question impact all of the students. Yes some of them might be asleep, but the whole point is that if you distribute your wording correctly, you can massively increase the thinking for minimal input from yourself. In essence (it's a slight exaggeration) you've saved yourself coming up with and asking 30 individual questions. Now multiply this across the whole of a lesson, and you've made your teaching efficient and maximised the learning by just redistributing your wording.

I'm not one for planning your questioning. In your training year you may be advised to always question your PP students or your lower prior achievers (or whichever group is fashionable at the time) but I think keeping it simple is better. All you are doing by pre-planning your targets is railroading your questioning and we all know that the efficiency of your teaching is reduced if you lose the ability to improvise, and if you have wasted time planning who you will ask questions and you don't then that's a further unnecessary increase in workload. My approach is that everyone is fair game. If you get your distribution spread and wording out right, the whole class is involved anyway.

## Commonality of language

Questioning doesn't need to be a mystical process. In fact, the more transparent it is, the more likely students are to opt in and respond. With that said, you shouldn't avoid using language that is challenging or phrases that trigger deeper thinking. A common language or a shared understanding of words is a great way to make students feel comfortable with the questions they are being asked to answer.

A good point to start is the action words you choose to use when you ask questions. Do you know what you want back from the students? I mean do they know what you're actually asking them to do and do you? Making your words very clear from the outset is key. Think about the kinds of questions you ask and model how you respond to them. By doing this, you show students how to respond to specific phrases and action words. You can then couple these to exam questions and further integrate good practice into verbal responses. The idea of knowing and showing how you expect questions to be answered saves you the awkward process of constantly correcting students and it also saves any consolidation of misconceptions, because you can guarantee if they respond incorrectly verbally, their written responses will reflect this too.

Teaching talk explicitly is something we have explored earlier in this book, but consolidating and linking it to questioning is also very important. Vocalisation of concepts is one thing, but doing it in response to unplanned stimulus is a challenge. You can ensure that your questioning is effective by using simple questioning frames that you share with your classes. The example below is a way in which you can engage the learners in your class through disambiguating the expectation for the vocalisation of the response. Like any good scaffolding, this needs to be gradually removed, but creating a commonality of language means that students feel safer and more confident to engage with the questions you ask.

## Using the right type of question

I don't think there is a teacher who hasn't heard of Bloom's Taxonomy (1956)... it's the basis for a lot of the training still given to ITT trainees. Its foundation is that questioning can be broken into a number of levels and these levels can be accessed using various different phrases and words. In a number of ways it's a great introduction to questioning but for me implies totally the wrong thing, predominantly that there is a hierarchy as to which questions are more valuable than others. In my world, all questions are equal and every type has a time and a place. The misconception that has arisen and that continues to be spread (normally using annoyingly small laminated cards that are treasury tagged together) is that questions lower down on the hierarchy are lower order and should therefore be aimed at certain students whereas higher order questions should be aimed at others... give me a break, how can you evaluate if you can't remember? Is evaluating easier than remembering? Can you remember every word you've read in a book? No, but I bet you can evaluate it. Still think that the hierarchy is a good way to pitch your questioning?

Bloom's Taxonomy should be a circle really. It is a great resource for helping teachers to reflect on the ways in which they can get students to apply different skills through questioning, but it is by no means a tool which should be used to differentiate challenge in questioning. Sticking to the ideal that "harder questions" are evaluation questions will hinder the effectiveness of your questioning and may result in disengagement. You need to ensure that you have a number of strategies in place to vary your questioning, but things that actually reduce your workload, not increase it.

Questioning exercises have always taken a number of formats depending on the most recent fad. I personally would advise avoiding like the plague any approaches like lollipop sticks and questioning tasks that involve you cutting up pieces of paper. Anything that takes you time to produce outside the classroom increases your workload and like we've said, unless it's having a direct impact on the learning, it's not time well spent. Spending your time ensuring that you have planned your questioning at the right time or brushing up on your subject knowledge is a much better use of time than making gimmicks.

There are a number of different types of questions that you can use when you are teaching and knowing the pros and cons of each approach can help you become a lot more efficient and selective about when you choose to use each, because getting it right can mean the difference between progress and confusion.

### Closed questions

- A question with a binary response.

Although for years closed questions got a lot of bad press, they're making a firm comeback with the rise in popularity of recall and retrieval practice. Closed questions are great for starting activities and the recalling of key ideas and facts. In addition they can create quite a pace for questioning and also allow for anchor points to be established before discussion is furthered. What annoys me about closed questioning is that teachers often use them on their "less able" students in order to simply tick a box – they've responded, move on. Don't fall into this trap. Consider varying your recipients when it comes to closed questions as it can quickly become a bad habit of asking the same students these questions. Additionally, if used in isolation, closed questions don't encourage a huge amount of discussion, so handle them with care and pepper them in conjunction with other approaches to get the most from them.

## Open questions

- A question with an unrestricted response.

Open questions are the other end of the spectrum to the above. Open questions can be great for discussion and allow a real in depth, rich discussion around a topic… assuming the previous learning is consolidated. Due to the nature of the question, there is less likely to be a wrong or right answer (specifically) so the likelihood is that responses to these questions will be more in-depth as they require a lot more reasoning to be answered. I suppose some may claim that "higher order skills" are required to answer these kind of questions, and to a degree there is some truth there, but again, don't fall into the trap of limiting the students who you give the opportunity to answer these questions. Avoid using open questions to check recall of knowledge, it's a long-winded way round and isn't an efficient use of time.

## Socratic questions

- Systematic, disciplined and deep questions, normally focused on fundamental concepts, principles, theories, issues or problems.

This approach is based on the idea that thinking has structured logic, and allows underlying thoughts to be questioned (Paul & Binker 1990, p. 360).

When I first read about Socratic reasoning and Socratic questioning, I was really hungover in a lecture theatre in Newcastle and even then, the concept blew my mind. Obviously, this approach is named after the Ancient Greek philosopher Socrates and is loosely based on his approach to questioning. The approach utilises the teacher's ability to facilitate challenging, rigorous and insightful questioning and dialogue among pupils. The idea is that the teacher sets up and manipulates encouraging the pupils to challenge and evaluate views and ideas put forth by their peers or by the teacher. For me, the main advantages of this type of classroom dialogue is that it encourages critical thinking and builds on the skills required for self-efficacy when it comes to building an argument. With the right teaching, the Socratic style of questioning can be developed into a pupil-centred approach to learning. This is massively powerful in that students can begin to address the misconceptions of others in the class… which reduces your workload a lot. The warning is, of course, that you near some clear expectations around this type of questioning or it falls flat on its face. Moreover, you need to train (and yes I just said train) your students how to effectively engage with this kind of approach.

### Hinge questions

- A question used at a pivotal point in learning – normally at the end of a topic.

I think applying and exploiting hinge questions is a skill that is hugely underrated. For early career teachers, taking the time to ascertain if pupils are ready to move from one topic to another is vital for you to truly make your teaching smarter. Hinge questions can be the difference between success and confusion and are a great way for you to check that your students have taken away the key learning points from your teaching. A way that you can do this in a low-workload way is through multiple choice questioning. These questions can then be coupled with others to give a better insight into understanding and what learning has taken place. Hinge questions are very helpful, but they do have some drawbacks, namely when they are used. Often hinge questions are used at the end of sequence of learning when learning is freshest. The Ebbinghaus forgetting curve (1880) reminds us that this kind of testing needs to be spaced or the results that the checking yields may be misleading. Pashler et al. (2007) suggest that waiting 10–20% of the time towards when the information will be needed is the optimum time for a single review. Regardless of how you use hinge questions, remember to factor in when you are checking knowledge, as it may not reflect true learning.

## Leading questions

- A question that prompts or encourages an answer in some way.

A lot of teachers have a natural ability to use leading questions; I think if we didn't we'd go round in circles sometimes. Leading questions are designed to direct pupils towards the answer or to engage pupils in discussion and depending on how much leading is used, the difficulty can be adjusted for the student giving the answer. Using some of Lemov's (2015) *Teach Like a Champion* approaches, teachers can ensure that they maintain the level of challenge required for learning, but assist and hint towards students to help them overcome the proverbial brick wall. Break It Down, Call and Response, and Pepper are but to name a few of the amazing approaches mentioned in the book. If you haven't already, take a look at how Lemov suggests increasing participation ratio through questioning. He's a genius (love you Doug).

Leading questions are great for helping students develop their skills of deduction and allow the teacher to build up a positive feeling around questioning where students don't feel isolated and fearing failure. Moreover, the additional element of control allows you to steer the conversation and dictate the pace. If time is tight and you have an agenda, leading questions can make your questioning phases more efficient, but don't overuse them. Students are astute when it comes to how much help they'll get and if they become reliant on your input, they won't be firing on all cylinders – they'll just think that you'll help them straightaway. It also can mask misconceptions that have arisen or are arising because the students uses your hint to guess at the right answer.

## Probing questions

- A question used to help learners think more deeply.

A way that you can add some real depth to learning and discussion around a topic is through simple probing questions. These questions allow teachers and pupils to dig deeper into the topics without a huge amount of additional brain power being used on formulating questions. Ideas and opinions can be drilled down on through individual words, "How?" "Why?" etc. Probing questions may be asked as a sequence of questions following a more open response. I like to funnel probing questions by starting off broad and then taking my time to refine the discussion by probing in a set order. The routine of this helps the students with their formulation of written responses as I follow the same framework. Probing (generally) encourages a level of deeper thinking but can be intimidating for some students as it requires them to think quickly. You need to balance your workload when questioning with the efficiency of the learning. Too many probing questions can actually detract from the original question stem if you aren't careful and, moreover, these questions often mean that you lose control of where the discussion goes.

## Rhetorical questions

- A question that requires no direct answer.

Sometimes, students don't even need to answer your questions. It may seem counterintuitive, but questioning can be just as powerful if you get no response. By getting students to question themselves, they are able to reflect in a way that is low-threat to them. In addition, you can coach and support their learning without taking away from them working. One of the issues with rhetorical questions is that it is difficult to ascertain if they have had any impact on the learning unless coupled with other approaches that encourage vocalisation.

## Multiple choice questions (MCQs)

- A type of question with multiple given responses, one of which is correct.

I debated folding these questions in with closed questions, but I thought better of it. A well-formulated MCQ test can be a phenomenally useful tool if designed correctly, especially when testing retrieval knowledge. Writing effective MCQs is an art in itself and would require a fair chunk of explanation, but once you have spent the time designing an effective sequence of questions, you can very easily highlight misconceptions in learning. MCQs need to be sufficient in that the test has to be challenging to the person being examined while also assessing knowledge and understanding, so the answer can be obvious or deductible from guesswork. Avoid the *Who Wants To Be a Millionaire*-style approach, as this isn't gathering reliable data on what's been learnt. Multiple choice questioning can vary from straightforward to very difficult.

Brame (2013) concisely highlights some of the factors teachers can consider when writing MCQs. It is mostly common sense in terms of what you need to do, but actually doing it for every question can be quite a skill. If you get your test right, you'll get reliable, accurate and clear data about learning and student knowledge. Tips from Brame include the following:

- The stem should always be a question or a partial statement.
- The question/statement should be meaningful and not contain irrelevant material (also avoid any inaccuracies in spelling and grammar).
- All alternatives to the correct response should be plausible. The function of the incorrect alternatives is to serve as distractors.
- Alternatives should be stated clearly and concisely. They should be mutually exclusive and should be homogenous in content.
- Alternatives should be free from clues about which response is correct. The alternatives should be presented in a logical order.

- The alternatives "all of the above" and "none of the above" should not be used.

- Avoid complex multiple choice items, in which some or all of the alternatives consist of different combinations of options.

- Keep the specific content of items independent of one another – avoid questions relying on correctly answering other questions or previous questions hinting at the answers to others.

I was never convinced about multiple choice questioning as I was a questioning snob until somebody showed me the results these things can yield and how helpful they can be with regard to identifying patterns in gaps in student knowledge. Of course, these types of questions have their limitations with regard to the fact that they don't allow for any testing beyond surface knowledge (except when you go really extreme) and also, students can guess at the answer, giving you potentially flawed data regardless of how bullet-proof your preparation is... but keep an open mind as to how much this type of questioning can reduce your workload and increase the efficiency of learning, especially facts and simple ideas.

## Calling for response

We've touched on the ideas of participation and thinking ratio and the importance of ensuring that these are kept to the maximum with regard to the time and effort spent by the teacher. What I'm going to suggest now is controversial in some ways and you may have to take a moment to put this down and mutter to yourself about my insanity, but the best way to ensure this is to go full-on cold-call questioning. Yep, you heard me, no hands up at all. Taking full control of the questioning in your classroom means that you are always able to drive the momentum in a way that engages the maximum amount of students. It also removes your prejudice with regard to hands up. Hands up limits your pool of potential answering students and it can really slow down the questioning phases in your lessons. It also creates more extraneous load for you. You have a working memory too remember and coming up with a question and having additional variables thrown in the mix makes questioning even harder. Have a go at doing cold-call for a whole lesson and see how you get on. Trust me.

Being adaptable and fluid is something that early career teachers lack when it comes to questioning. Forget asking a series of longer questions, we don't want children being overloaded with burdensome phrases. Instead, ask one question and then use this as a springboard for a series of simple questions. The art of simplicity allows students to respond almost instinctively to the response of their peers and this collaborative responding can have a notable impact on how students are able to tease out details from each other's answers. Take the same example from earlier and think about these additions:

Teacher: What's the capital of England? Josh

Josh: [Answer]

Teacher: What about Wales? Megan

Megan: [Answer]

Teacher: How are the cities different? Eli

Eli: [Answer]

Teacher: Agree or disagree – Emily?

Emily: [Answer]

Teacher: Take a point and elaborate. Tyler

Tyler: [Answer]

Teacher: So where would you rather live? James

Etc.

Bouncing questions around doesn't need to be clumpy and ever-increasing in sophistication. If you get the wording right, you can cover a number of skills and really engage the students and when coupled with a written exercise, this type of questioning can model a strong response if handled correctly, again further reducing your workload in the classroom and freeing your time up for other teaching activities.

## Set expectations around questioning

You can ask the best questions in the world, in the most effective manner with perfect wording, but if you get nothing back, the process becomes a time pit and ends up in an awkward mess. I'm sure there have been times where you are firing out the questions and you've hit the blank wall of refusal. I think it's a kind of teenage protest sometimes. If a class has a collective refusal, they can make a lot of work for you (and they know it), so how can you avoid this? It comes down to your expectations around questioning.

Creating a culture of trust is paramount and from the outset, ensuring that your learning space is safe for students to respond makes questioning much less of a threat. Equally, distributing your questions fairly and evenly means that learners are more likely to feel involved and not "picked on". If you teach lower prior achievers, don't just focus on motivating them with empty praise, this will have a near zero effect on their learning (Gorard et al., 2012). Instead, consider your questioning approach to ensure the difficulty is desirable and allow them to succeed by asking the right questions in the right way. Their motivation will increase through the success and the praise can be saved for a more deserving purpose.

Pitching your questioning effectively is also a factor that contributes to engagement. Using the most desirable difficulty for each individual means that there is a sufficient level of challenge, with a high chance of success with some effort. And that's what you want to work towards – students wanting to be questioned so they can stretch their understanding. Building up the confidence of learners by building their resilience and reconditioning their ideas around the concept of failure is also paramount to engaging students with questioning. Using approaches such as Doug Lemov's (2015) Break It Down, you can shave away difficulty one layer at a time to help students answer a question by giving them hints and pointers, but without giving them the answer. Little approaches like this show it's okay to not get the answer right straightaway. In fact, when utilised and delivered effectively, the teacher is able to model how students can strip these layers away themselves in order to become more self-sufficient. By creating an expectation and routine about how to break down questions, teachers can encourage a higher level of self-efficacy.

- Are your expectations around questioning explicit and clear?
- Do you use a range of questioning approaches?
- Why do you use each type of questioning?
- Can you explain the impact of the way in which you question and when one approach may be more effective than another in your context?
- How do you currently question children with regard to selecting them?
- What can you do to reduce your workload around questioning?

# 8 Reflecting

By now, I hope you've had the chance to reflect on your teaching and how you can, could or may be able to reduce your workload. I wish it was as easy as waving a magic wand, but like most things in the world, it isn't!

## Plan/prepare/implement/reflect/repeat

Changing various elements of your teaching overnight isn't a sustainable reality. For you to make yourself truly effective and efficient, you need to make sure you plan your changes in way that allows you to no become overburdened. Reducing workload shouldn't be a stressful business, but it may take some time to embed certain approaches in your teaching. They say you should never share a stage with animals or children on account of their unpredictability, but unfortunately, you don't have a huge amount of choice. The children may be unpredictable and they may wander off the proverbial stage occasionally, so remember that change takes time, and that's totally okay.

    Carefully plan what you will change and when you will do it. It may be at the start of a term, the start of a week or even the start of tomorrow. Whenever you decide to implement new approaches or make modifications to your existing practice, make sure that you have fully thought it through and are comfortable with how and why you are making the changes. Don't just reflect on this book and see it as a quick-fix guide, for you to implement any of the strategies mentioned, or in fact any strategy you ever come across, you must understand and believe in it. Children are astute beasts who have exceptional bull detectors, and if you're serious about reducing your workload, you must be brought into your own changes. A half-hearted implementation or a toe in the water approach will inevitably result in failure – you want to give each change you make a good chance of succeeding. If it doesn't succeed because of the audience, that's one thing but if it's because of your approach, you need to be aware of this.

If you take nothing more away from this book than the importance of being reflective, then you've still equipped yourself with the most effective tool you can have for being a teacher. You must always continue to look at how you are working in order for you to improve. You don't need to be critical, but you must critique your practice. As the spotlight moves away from you after your training year and your NQT year, it is easy to allow yourself to get comfortable. They prying eyes may only come to your classroom once a year and between those times, the kingdom is yours. Make sure that you don't fall into a rut. Evaluate and forensically diagnose your successes, failures, speed bumps and elations and make sure that you know what practice is effective and what is not. Reflective makes you effective and this is what will make you exceptional in the classroom.

It can be tough going back over something you've proactively changed, but you must. Reflecting is one thing, but continual improvement comes from a cycle of evaluation and reapplying. Once you start to reduce your workload, you'll become more informed about your approaches and why they are or aren't effective. After a period of time, you may be able to refine them even further to reduce your workload even more. You must embrace change and see it as something that helps, not hinders.

## Keep on keeping on

Although it may not always be spoken about explicitly, it's in the post-training years where much of your real learning will happen.

Stick with it and remember that the more you can do to reduce your workload, the more time you have to, well, be like normal people. You need to thrive and not just survive

Keeping it simple will mean that you have time for yourself and time to focus on your students. Decluttering your workspace and you practice should leave more room for you to do your job. The trick is to maintain your reflection when it comes to your teaching. If you make a load of changes to streamline your practice and then two or six months later you allow your workload to start creeping up, you'll find yourself back to square one when it comes to stress. Remember that reflective = effective – don't take your eye off the proverbial mirror and make sure you stay aware of what you are doing in (and out of) the classroom

Teaching is a highly demanding job. There are times when the pressure will feel too much, but the thing to remember is that you will make it through. There's that feeling of dread that you haven't done enough, that there's something else that needs to be done. But you must remember, there is always something else that could be done, regardless of how effective or amazing you are. Teaching is profoundly unique job that weirdly has very few rules regarding how you go about your job. As a result, there's always something more you can do.

How can you get a balance? If the dread ever begins to set in, ask yourself these questions: What is most important? What is my priority? Focus on those, and use your time effectively. It won't always get rid of the dread, but it'll certainly help you put things into perspective.

For all the hard work, you will be substantially rewarded – possibly financially and certainly emotionally. Sometimes it's a smile from a pupil when they finally understand a concept, sometimes it's a phone call from a parent, and sometimes it will be on results day, when you see the tears of joy as a young person gets the grades they need to get into their dream college or university. You get tasters of these rewards throughout your training, and when you get into the classroom as a qualified teacher, they are amplified massively. People will often ask, "Why do you teach?" This is most likely the reason. Cherish it and let it motivate you. When times are tough, just think back to why you got into teaching and focus on the positives.

It all seems quite straightforward during training and your first years teaching. Here is a specification – learn it, make lessons for it, and prepare pupils for the test. The sands seem solid and it isn't until they begin shifting that you realise your foundation may not be as solid as you thought. Specifications change regularly and often these amendments require a significant amount of rewriting and relearning. It's a necessary evil due to the fluidity of education, the goal posts will move, and you need to ensure that you are adaptable. You'll pick up a lot in your first years teaching, but you never really stop learning. Don't let curriculum changes worry you. Are they always for the better? No. We all know that. See spec changes as a challenge or a refresher, not as a hindrance.

There will come a time where you get a few years into your teaching and you'll hit a lull. Regardless of how much you deny it, it will come. For some it may last a long time; for you, make sure it doesn't. It isn't intentional, just something that happens. It can be disheartening when you just can't seem to get yourself out of that rut of tiredness and repetition, but don't let it beat you. If you feel yourself entering a lull, get yourself out of it before you get stuck. Be proactive. Ask colleagues if you can do some observations. Maybe get involved with your institution's training programme, or ask to be put on an external course. Keeping yourself fresh is the key to avoiding lulls in your career. Picking up knowledge from others is hugely rewarding, and mixing up your classroom practice will ensure that you continually improve your teaching. Lulls occur when teachers get complacent, and that complacency can lead to all sorts of other issues in the classroom.

## Read up

Teaching smart is about filtering out the white noise and focusing on what is important in the classroom. I'm certainly not an all-knowing oracle when it comes to teaching and there is no way that the contents of this book are going to be the only ways in which you can reduce your workload.

Keep current and read up on what others are doing. Blogs, teaching magazines and websites are the obvious suggestions, but Twitter and

Facebook both also offer their own levels of support for teachers. Networking and reading about the experiences of others can be a huge factor in continuing to reduce your workload.

Just as you are hopefully trying to be in your own practice, be reflective when it comes to new ideas. Use your teacher sense and decide if the approaches being talked about will help you make life easier or if in fact they are a fad that will actually cause you more hassle in the long run. Don't take everything you read for gospel, especially the things written by people so far detached from the classroom that they can even tell you the last time they were in front of a class of 30. Read as much as you can by teachers and people who actually spend time doing the things they are writing about. I've tried to stay relatively uncontroversial through the entirety of this text, but you must always think about who is tell you what, and whether their "25 years of being a head teacher" is as positive as the fact they haven't set foot in front of students in ten years (if not more.) Anyone can talk the talk when it comes to writing about best practice, but can they walk the walk? Be selective and ask yourself (or them if you can) if they can demonstrate what they are preaching.

## Manage stress

Too much stress is not conducive to a good working environment. You need to regulate your stress levels and in order to be effective, but this, of course, is much easier said than done. Stress manifests itself in a number of ways and due to the emotional nature of teaching, I think it's almost impossible to remove stress from the equation. Some short-term stress can be motivational and can actually help with the effective completion of tasks, but prolonged stress can lead to a reduction in efficiency and a lot of unfavourable side-effects.

As teachers, we need to look after ourselves and others around us. Knowing your own limits is important and having the awareness to know when you need to rest, stop or step away from a situation is often distorted by the pressing issues that you face. With this in mind, looking after yourself is paramount. Eating, sleeping and exercising should be seriously high on your priority list and be coming in well above marking and planning. Additionally, taking the time to look out for each other should also be high on the list of priorities. A school or a department can't be run solely by one person (okay, I know sometimes it is!) so don't forget that you are part of a team, be that in your subject, in the school or in a trust.

A wise person once told me: "Be a radiator, not a drain." I don't remember which wise person said it, but it's done me well with regard to how I go about my day. You have your stresses and other people have theirs, make sure that you aren't adding to anybody else's stress by being negative. Negativity breeds negativity and in teaching, this can be poisonous. Be the shining light and not the plug hole.

## Final words

Wisdom in this world comes in many forms. Like I said at the start, I'm no academic, I'm just a classroom teacher who was a bit sick of doing stuff just because I was trained to do it that way or because I was told it was what I needed to do. Teaching is a profession in which we must always ask, "Why?" If we don't, we run the risk of being swept up in the wake of one of the highest-pressure jobs going.

Workload is a tameable beast, no matter your setting or context. You can make adjustments to your teaching to make your life easier, there are no two ways around it. Even now, I am making adjustments weekly to try and reduce my workload even further while staying as, if not more, effective in the classroom.

Your first years teaching don't necessarily define you, but they are certainly the time during which the wheat is separated from the chaff. Teaching offers a promising career and years (and years) of job satisfaction. Getting yourself through the first stage of your career isn't easy, so do everything you can to reduce the strain. We need teachers like you in the profession, because without you, the school world will be a much darker place... and more of us will have to do cover.

Best of luck. Keep fighting the good fight.

# References

Baddeley, A.D., & Longman, D.J.A. (1978). The influence of length and frequency of training session on the rate of learning to type. *Ergonomics*, 21, 627–635.

Ball, D.L. (1991). Research on teaching mathematics: Making subject matter knowledge part of the equation. In J. Brophy (Ed.), *Advances in research on teaching* (Vol. 2, pp. 1–48). Greenwich, CT: JAI Press Inc.

Bellon, J.J., Bellon, E.C., & Blank, M.A. (1991). *Teaching from a research knowledge base: A development and renewal process*. Facsimile edition. New Jersey: Prentice Hall.

Bjork, R.A. (1994). Memory and metamemory considerations in the training of human beings. In J. Metcalfe & A. Shimamura, *Metacognition: Knowing about knowing*. Cambridge, MA: MIT Press.

Bjork, E.L., & Bjork, R.A. (2011). Making things hard on yourself, but in a good way: Creating desirable difficulties to enhance learning. In M.A. Gernsbacher, R.W. Pew, L.M. Hough, J.R. Pomerantz (Eds.) & FABBS Foundation, *Psychology and the real world: Essays illustrating fundamental contributions to society* (pp. 56–64). New York: Worth Publishers.

Bjork, R.A., & Bjork, E.L. (1992). A new theory of disuse and an old theory of stimulus fluctuation. In A. Healy, S. Kosslyn, & R. Shiffrin (Eds.), *From learning processes to cognitive processes: Essays in Honor of William K. Estes* (Vol. 2, pp. 35–67). Hillsdale, NJ: Erlbaum.

Bourdieu, P. (1973). *Cultural reproduction and social reproduction in knowledge, education and cultural change*. London: Tavistock.

Bourdieu, P. (1977). *Outline of a theory of practice*. Cambridge: Cambridge University Press.

Bourdieu, P. (1984). *Distinction: a social critique of the judgement of taste*. London: Routledge.

Bourdieu, P. ([1986] 1997). Forms of capital. In A. Halsey, H. Lauder, P. Brown & A. Wells (Eds.), *Education: culture, economy and society*. Oxford & New York: Oxford University Press.

Brame, C. (2013). Writing good multiple choice test questions. Retrieved from: https://cft.vanderbilt.edu/guides-sub-pages/writing-good-multiple-choice-test-questions/ (accessed 20 October 2019).

Brophy, J., & Good, T. (1986). Teacher behavior and student achievement. In M. Wittrock (Ed.), *Handbook of research on teaching* (pp. 328–375). New York: Macmillan.

Butler, R. (1987). Task-involving and ego-involving properties of evaluation: Effects of different feedback conditions on motivational perceptions, interest, and performance. *Journal of Educational Psychology*, 79(4), 474–482.

Bye, J. (2011). Desirable difficulties in the classroom: When learning, how matters as much as what. *Psychology Today*. Retrieved from: www.psychologytoday.com/gb/blog/all-about-addiction/201105/desirable-difficulties-in-the-classroom (accessed 20 January 2020).

Coe, R., Aloisi, C., Higgins, S., & Major, L.E. (2014). *What makes great teaching? Review of the underpinning research*. London: Sutton Trust.

Danielson, C. (2007). *Enhancing professional practice: A framework for teaching*. Alexandria, VA: ASCD.

Danielson, C., & McGreal, T.L. (2000). *Teacher evaluation to enhance professional practice*. Alexandria, VA: ASCD.

Davenport, B., & Scott, S.J. (2015). *The 10-minute declutter: The stress-free habit of simplifying your home*. CreateSpace Independent Publishing Platform.

Dempster, F.N. (1990). The spacing effect: A case study in the failure to apply the results of psychological research. *American Psychologist*, 43, 627–634.

Dweck, C.S. (1999). Caution – praise can be dangerous. *American Educator*, Spring, pp. 4–9.

Dweck, C.S. (2012). *Mindset: How you can fulfil your potential*. London: Constable & Robinson.

Fisher, A.V., Godwin, K.E., & Seltman, H. (2014). Visual environment, attention allocation, and learning in young children: When too much of a good thing may be bad. *Psychological Science*, 25(7), 1362–1370.

Gorard, S., See, B.H., & Davies, P. (2012). *The impact of attitudes and aspirations on educational attainment and participation*. York: Joseph Rowntree Foundation.

Hattie, J. (2012). *Visible learning for teachers*. London: Routledge.

Hattie, J., & Timperley, H. (2007). The power of feedback. *Review of Educational Research*, 77(1), 81–112.

Higgins, S., Katsipataki, M., Kokotsaki, D., Coleman, R., Major, L.E., & Coe, R. (2013). *The Sutton Trust-Education Endowment Foundation Teaching and Learning Toolkit*. London: Education Endowment Foundation.

Hirsch, E.D., Kett, J.F., & Trefil, J.S. (1988). *Cultural literacy: What every American needs to know*. New York: Vintage Books.

Holton, D. (2009). Cognitive Load Theory: Failure? Retrieved from: https://edtechdev.wordpress.com/2009/11/16/cognitive-load-theory-failure/ (accessed 24 June 2019).

James, M., & Pollard, A. (2011). TLRP's ten principles for effective pedagogy: Rationale, development, evidence, argument and impact. *Research Papers in Education*, 26(3), 275–328.

Kirschner, P.A., Sweller, J., & Clark, R.E. (2006). Why minimal guidance during instruction does not work: An analysis of the failure of constructivist, discovery, problem-based, experiential, and inquiry-based teaching. *Educational Psychologist*, 41(2), 75–86.

Kluger, A.N., & DeNisi, A. (1998). Feedback interventions: Toward the understanding of a double-edged sword. *Current Directions in Psychological Science*, 7, 67–72.

Lemov, D. (2015). *Teach like a champion 2.0: 62 techniques that put students on the path to college*. San Francisco, CA: Jossey Bass.

McColskey, W., & Leary, M.R. (1985). Differential effects or norm-referenced and self-referenced feedback on performance expectancies, attribution, and motivation. *Contemporary Educational Psychology*, 10, 275–284.

McDaniel, M.A., Hines, R.J., Waddill, P.J., & Einstein, G.O. (1994). What makes folk tales unique: Content familiarity, causal structure, scripts, or superstructures? *Journal of Experimental Psychology: Learning, Memory, and Cognition*, 20, 169–184.

McNamara, D.S., Kintsch, E., Songer, N.B., & Kintsch, W. (1996). Are good texts always better? Interactions of text coherence, background knowledge, and levels of understanding in learning from text. *Cognition and Instruction*, 14, 1–43.

OECD (2015). *Annual education report*. Retrieved from: www.oecd.org/education/education-at-a-glance-2015.htm (accessed 27 January 2020).

Pashler, H., Rohrer, D., Cepeda, N.J., & Carpenter, S.K. (2007). Enhancing learning and retarding forgetting: Choices and consequences. *Psychonomic Bulletin & Review*, 14(2), 187–193.

Paul, R., & Binker, A.J. (1990). *Critical thinking: What every person needs to survive in a rapidly changing world*. Tomales, CA: Foundation for Critical Thinking.

Reif, F. (2010). *Applying cognitive science to education: Thinking and learning in scientific and other complex domains*. Cambridge, MA: MIT Press.

Riener, C., & Willingham, D. (2010). The myth of learning styles. *Change: The Magazine of Higher Learning*, 42(5), 32–35.

Roediger, H.L., III, & Karpicke, J.D. (2006). The power of testing memory: Basic research and implications for educational practice. *Perspectives on Psychological Science*, 1, 181–120.

Rosenshine, B. (2010). *Principles of instruction*. Geneva: International Bureau of Education.

Rosenshine, B. (2012). Principles of instruction: Research based principles that all teachers should know. *American Educator*, Spring 2012. Retrieved from: www.aft.org/pdfs/americaneducator/spring2012/Rosenshine.pdf (accessed 20 January 2020).

Salles, D. (2016). *The slightly awesome teacher*. UK: John Catt Educational.

Shank, P. (2017). Science of learning 101: Why learning should be hard. Retrieved from: http://bit.ly/2Kt6Fzi (accessed 20 January 2020).

Smith, S.M., Glenberg, A., & Bjork, R.A. (1978). Environmental context and human memory. *Memory & Cognition*, 6, 342–353.

Son, S.-H.C., & Strasser, K. (2002). *Direct and indirect influences of SES on home literacy activities and kindergarten reading skills: Evidence from early childhood longitudinal studies*. Paper presented at the 2002 National Association for the Education of Young Children Annual Conference, 20–23 November, New York.

Sweller, J. (1988). Cognitive load during problem solving: Effects on learning. *Cognitive Science*, 12(2), 257–285.

Sweller, J., Van Merriënboer, J., & Paas, F. (1998). Cognitive architecture and instructional design. *Educational Psychology Review*, 10(3), 251–296.

Sylva, K., Melhuish, E., Sammons, P., Siraj-Blatchford, I., and Taggart, B. (2004). *The effect of provision of pre-school education 3–11 project (EPPE 3–11): Final report*. Nottingham: Department for Education and Skills.

Sylva, K., Melhuish, E., Sammons, P., Siraj-Blatchford, I., and Taggart, B. (2008). *Final report from the primary phase: Pre-school, school and family influences on children's development during Key Stage 2 (7–11)*, DfE RR 061. Nottingham: Department for Education.

Thaler, R.H., & Sunstein, C.R. (2010). *Nudge: Improving decisions about health, wealth and happiness*. Concordville, PA: Soundview Executive Book Summaries.

Thom, J. (2018). *Slow teaching*. Ipswich: John Catt Publishing.

Willingham, D.T. (2008). What will improve a student's memory? *American Educator*, 32(4), 17–25.

# Index

assessment 10, 75, 87, 89

behaviour 16, 33–40, 59–69
Bjork, R. 14, 20, 95
Bourdieu, P. 25

circulating 39–42, 80, 87
classroom layout 30, 41
cognitive load theory 14–17, 22, 56
collaboration 27, 31, 49, 57–58, 89, 105
commonality of language 69, 92, 96–97
consistency 9, 36, 53, 57, 60–62, 65–66, 72
cultural capital 24–28
cultural literacy 24
curriculum 24, 26, 53, 112

data 78, 103–104
desirable difficulty 17, 20–22, 52–54, 69, 95, 106
desks 29–33, 36–42, 65, 71, 87
differentiation 32, 47–48
displays 30–31, 35–39, 43, 49, 73
Dweck, C.S. 67–68

errors 52–54, 75–79, 85
examples 23, 52, 54
exemplars 35, 53
expectations: behaviour 35–38; high expectations 59–60; learning 60–61; and parents 71–72; setting expectations 60–66; talking about 48–52; tasks 52–64; of teachers 72–74
extraneous load 16, 19, 31, 78, 104

feedback: effective feedback 56, 69, 75–79, 92; live feedback 42, 81–84; peer feedback 87–89; whole class 84–87

group work 31–34, 49, 51
guided instruction 22

Hattie, J. 57, 76, 88
homework 71

independent practice 20, 40, 46, 79
intrinsic load 14–15

knowledge 8, 14–16, 22, 25–28, 46–47, 50–58, 65–68
knowledge organisers 71

leadership 7, 58, 72
Lemov, D. 40, 53, 101, 106

marking 4, 41–42, 73, 75–87, 113
memory 14–16, 22, 48, 91, 104
misconceptions 38, 40–48, 52–55, 69, 75–89, 95, 97, 100, 102
modelling 42, 46, 50, 52–55, 62, 80
monitoring tasks 79–81

no hands up 104

parents 70–72
planning: classroom 12, 16–19, 21; expectations 64–65; lessons 45–58, 88; misconceptions 79
praise 67–71, 106

questioning: approaches to questioning 51, 65, 82, 91–104; cold call questioning 51, 104–105; distribution 32, 94–96; expectations of questioning 104–107; student questioning 26–27

119

research 6, 9, 11, 13, 18, 23
Rosenshine, B. 17–20, 46

social capital 25
stress 38–39, 111, 113–114
subject knowledge 53, 93–94, 98
Sweller, J. 14–16

talk 25–26, 48–52, 61, 68
teacher retention 9
Thom, J. 38

Willingham, D. 47, 91